I0410604

ERITREA: A NEGLECTED REGIONAL THREAT

HEARING

BEFORE THE

SUBCOMMITTEE ON AFRICA, GLOBAL HEALTH, GLOBAL HUMAN RIGHTS, AND INTERNATIONAL ORGANIZATIONS

OF THE

COMMITTEE ON FOREIGN AFFAIRS HOUSE OF REPRESENTATIVES

ONE HUNDRED FOURTEENTH CONGRESS

SECOND SESSION

SEPTEMBER 14, 2016

Serial No. 114–237

Printed for the use of the Committee on Foreign Affairs

Available via the World Wide Web: http://www.foreignaffairs.house.gov/ or http://www.gpo.gov/fdsys/

U.S. GOVERNMENT PUBLISHING OFFICE

21–541PDF   WASHINGTON : 2016

For sale by the Superintendent of Documents, U.S. Government Publishing Office
Internet: bookstore.gpo.gov   Phone: toll free (866) 512–1800; DC area (202) 512–1800
Fax: (202) 512–2104   Mail: Stop IDCC, Washington, DC 20402–0001

CONTENTS

ERITREA: A NEGLECTED REGIONAL THREAT

WEDNESDAY, SEPTEMBER 14, 2016

House of Representatives,
Subcommittee on Africa, Global Health,
Global Human Rights, and International Organizations,
Committee on Foreign Affairs,
Washington, DC.

The subcommittee met, pursuant to notice, at 2:26 p.m., in room 2172 Rayburn House Office Building, Hon. Christopher H. Smith (chairman of the subcommittee) presiding.

Mr. SMITH. The subcommittee hearing will come to order, and welcome to all of our distinguished witnesses and also my good friend and colleague, the gentlelady from California.

In 1993, the citizens of Eritrea, then a province of Ethiopia, voted to become an independent nation. Ethiopia had annexed Eritrea in 1962 and its citizens no doubt believed that they were well on their way to controlling their own destiny.

Unfortunately, their hopes would soon be dashed. Elections have been repeatedly postponed and opposition political parties are no longer able to organize.

Those same initial hopes for democracy and good government in Eritrea were also held by the international community.

In March 1997, in a report by the U.S. Agency for International Development program in the country, the American aid agency had high praise for its collaboration with the government.

It said, in part, "Over the past year the young state of Eritrea continued its exciting and pace-setting experiment in nation building and similarly USAID Eritrea established itself as Eritrea's leading development partner."

Within a few years, however, the Government of Eritrea ended its relationship with USAID. But this decision was originally taken as a sign that the country was ready to become an example to the rest of the developing world by managing its own humanitarian needs.

Eritrea's Government instead merely became less open and when an east African drought occurred in 2011 we knew very little about how the people were faring.

Today, we know that two-thirds of Eritreans live on subsistence agriculture, which has had poor yields due to recurring droughts and low productivity. What we also know is that Eritrea's citizens are living under a regime that does not honor human rights.

In June of this year, the U.N. Human Rights Council released a report that accused the government with a variety of violations including extrajudicial executions, torture, indefinitely prolonged national service and forced labor, sexual harassment, rape, and sexual servitude by state officials.

In its Trafficking in Persons Report released in June 2016, the State Department listed Eritrea as a Tier 3—that is the most egregious violator country—and stated that Eritrea is a source country for men, women, and children subjected to forced labor. The government did not investigate, prosecute, or convict trafficking offenders during the reporting year. The government demonstrated negligible efforts to identify and protect trafficking victims. The government maintained minimal efforts to prevent trafficking.

In their most recent international religious freedom report the State Department again listed Eritrea as a Country of Particular Concern, or a CPC country.

Moreover, the U.S. Commission on International Religious Freedom lists Eritrea as a Tier 1 Country of Particular Concern for its egregious religious freedom violations.

The government interferes with the internal affairs of registered religious groups and represses the religious liberty of those faith groups that refuses to register, such as Evangelical and Pentecostal Christians, Jehovah's Witnesses, and Muslims who do not follow the government-appointed head of the Islamic community.

Furthermore, the government has a record of arbitrarily arresting the believers and their leaders and reportedly tortures those in prolonged detention.

As a result of the authoritarian government sanctions, Eritrea is considered one of the world's fastest-emptying nations with about ½ million of the country's citizens having left their homes for often dangerous paths to freedom. An estimated 5,000 Eritreans leave their country each month.

On July 9, 2015, a hearing by our subcommittee on Africa refugees, John Stauffer, president of the American Team for Displaced Eritreans, told us that the government officials operated freely in eastern Sudan, arresting and bringing back to Eritrea those they considered high value targets among refugees, such as government officials or church leaders.

He also testified that refugees moving east may be kidnapped and extorted locally for a few thousand dollars or taken off to Egypt or Libya where they are abused. That abuse often included organ harvesting.

In the past year, the world has witnessed a flood of Eritrean refugees risking their lives on too often unseaworthy boats bound for Europe. The prevalence of Eritreans among refugees has been overshadowed by refugees from the Middle East, especially Syria.

The UK, one of the prime destinations for Eritrean refugees, apparently wanted to slow down the flow of Eritreans into the country. Earlier this year, the UK reduced the percentage of asylum claims from 95 percent to 28 percent.

Directly addressing the root causes of the flight of people who are voting with their feet, often at great risk, seems a better policy than trying to determine the final destination of Eritreans who feel forced to leave their homes. That means an enhanced level of communication between Eritrea's Government and the international community.

There have been quiet contacts between the government, the U.S. Government, and civil society. Today's hearing will examine how such contacts have developed. We hope the testimony in this hearing will answer some critical questions.

Can the United States form a relationship with a government it has under sanction? Does the dire situation in which Eritrea's people live require an alteration of U.S. policy? What would a change in policy mean for the international effort to hold Eritrea's Government responsible for blatant human rights violations?

Again, I want to thank our distinguished witnesses in advance for being here, including and especially the distinguished Assistant Secretary of State, Linda Thomas-Greenfield, who we'll get to shortly.

But I'd like to yield to my friend, the ranking member.

Ms. BASS. Thank you, Mr. Chair, and let me thank you for calling this hearing today. I think it is particularly important.

You mentioned the refugee crisis and we all know that the attention has been focused on refugees from Syria but we know the number of people that are also fleeing Eritrea and not getting the same level of attention.

I can't tell you how many times I have talked to folks from Ethiopia and Eritrea locally who always stop and say why don't you do hearings—why don't you do hearings on what is happening in Eritrea. So I think that this hearing is particularly timely and I appreciate you calling this today.

I will say that in preparing for the hearing a number of organizations—the Organization of Eritrean-Americans and several other organizations—are concerned and upset about why we are holding this hearing, taking the opposite point of view and saying that what we claim is happening in Eritrea is not and I don't know if on the second panel, not with the Assistant Secretary, but maybe someone could explain why there are so many people fleeing the country if what is being talked about around the world is in fact not the case.

Eritrea is known as a country that it is claimed is the most censured country in the world, has been cited repeatedly for its abysmal human rights record, and as you mentioned in terms of the issue of trafficking I think that all is widely known. And so the question is if this is so off why does the world view Eritrea in this way.

I'd like to ask the Assistant Secretary if she could share the administration's perspective regarding Eritrea's support of terrorism and the ongoing relevancy of the U.N. arms embargo and sanctions, whether the embargo and sanctions continue to be warranted and on what basis should there be consideration to eliminating the sanctions.

I am also interested in your assessment of the role of the E.U. and its development programs with Eritrea. I know part of this, especially the increase in aid, is to stem the emmigration. But I would like to know what your thoughts are on that.

And I am very interested in hearing witnesses representing the diaspora in the U.S. and what measures do these various diaspora groups support. Are they in support of a stronger relationship between Washington and Asmara or a continuation of the current approach.

Thank you, Mr. Chairman. I yield back.

Mr. SMITH. Thank you very, very much.

I would like to now introduce Ambassador Linda Thomas-Greenfield, a career member of the Foreign Service. She was sworn in on August 6, 2013, and is the Assistant Secretary for African affairs.

Prior to assuming her current position she led a team of about 400 employees who carried out personnel functions for the State Department's 70,000 strong workforce. Since beginning her Foreign Service career in 1982, she has risen through the ranks to the Minister Counselor level, serving in Jamaica, Nigeria, Gambia, Kenya, Pakistan, and the U.S. Mission to the U.N. and most recently as Ambassador to Liberia where she served from 2008 to 2012. I'd like to now yield the floor to the distinguished Assistant Secretary.

STATEMENT OF THE HONORABLE LINDA THOMAS-GREEN-FIELD, ASSISTANT SECRETARY, BUREAU OF AFRICAN AF-FAIRS, U.S. DEPARTMENT OF STATE

Ambassador THOMAS-GREENFIELD. Thank you, Mr. Chairman, and thank you, Ranking Member Bass, for inviting me today and providing the opportunity for us to testify on the situation in Eritrea, and I am pleased to have my colleague, Eric Whitaker, seated next to me.

Eric is the director of the Office of East African Affairs and he was just in Eritrea for about 2 months working as our Charge d'Affaires. So he may be able to give a little more depth to questions that you might have about the current situation in Eritrea.

After 25 years of independence, Eritrea today stands as a country best known for its emmigration, and I say that word specifically so there is no misunderstanding. It's known for its emmigration and its poor record on human rights.

Out of a population of approximately 3½ million people per U.N. estimates, an estimated 5,000 people a month flee the country. Many risk a perilous journey across Africa and across the Mediterranean at the hands of sometimes ruthless smugglers and in unsafe vessels.

The country is hemorrhaging its youth. In a country that has never known an election, Eritreans, as you said, Mr. Chairman, are voting with their feet. They are fleeing indefinite conscription into military or national service, religious persecution and other human rights violations, and economic hardships. These same conditions frame the United States' relationship with Eritrea.

In virtually every other country in Africa, including those with whom we have profound disagreements, we still seek to achieve partnerships across a range of shared global interests.

We provide billions in foreign assistance to support those partnerships formed to fight HIV/AIDS and malaria, to support education, to combat violent extremism, and to strengthen governance.

In Eritrea, that is not the case and that is because of the decisions of the Eritrean Government. In 2005, the Eritrean Government ordered USAID, other donors, international NGOs to leave the country.

Subsequently, it ordered our Embassy defense attache's office to close and as a result today we have no bilateral assistance, no military to military relationships, and since 2010 we have not had an Ambassador in Asmara.

This is not the relationship we desire. Eritrea is one of the poorest countries on Earth. It is located in a volatile and strategic neighborhood on the Red Sea.

But if Eritrea likes to portray itself as David and the United States as Goliath, I would argue that its wounds are largely self-inflicted and its slingshots hurl stones at its own people.

Up to 5,000 of them make this clear every single month, risking their lives rather than remaining in the country they love.

Eritrea's continuing torrent of immigration is no doubt driven in part by economic conditions. But it is the human rights records that push so many people to leave.

Over the past decade, the Eritrean Government has arbitrarily detained journalists, political opposition members, and others trying to express their reform minded to others who have tried to push for reforms.

In 2001, the government detained without charge a group of reform minded ministers and other prominent individuals who called for elections and implementation of the Constitution and many of these individuals remain in prison until today.

Almost all citizens with few exceptions are forced into indefinite conscription, into national service. In many cases they are separated from their families for years.

The government has imposed severe restrictions on the exercise and freedom of religion and belief and has subjected members of non-authorized religions to arbitrary detention and force recanting as a condition of release.

The government has singled out groups such as the Jehovah's Witnesses for particularly harsh treatment because of their members' refusal to bear arms in the independence struggle or to participate in national service.

Eritrean officials have long justified their poor human rights record and their large-scale militarization on an emergency, "No war, no peace," situation over the unresolved demarcation of their border with Ethiopia.

Eritrea has remained under a U.N.-imposed arms embargo and sanctions since 2009 for its actions that contributed to regional instability, including their support for al-Shabaab in Somalia.

In the last two annual reports, the U.N. Somalia-Eritrea Monitoring Group has not found evidence of ongoing support to al-Shabaab but Asmara has refused to allow the group to visit, to conduct investigations in Eritrea per its mandate and this has limited the U.N.'s ability to determine Eritrea's compliance with the sanctions regime.

Eritrea also continues to hold Djiboutian prisoners of war and is accused of fomenting unrest in neighboring countries.

For all these reasons, we have made it clear that turning a new page in the United States-Eritrea relationship first requires significant improvements in human rights and we have repeatedly called on the government to abide by its international human rights obligations, implement its own Constitution, hold national elections, honor its commitment to limit the duration of national service to 18 months, develop an independent and transparent judiciary, and release persons who have been arbitrarily detained.

We also continue to support the work of the Office of the U.N. High Commissioner for Human Rights, the U.N. Somalia-Eritrea Monitoring Group, as well as other international efforts to make progress.

And, surprisingly, there has been some progress albeit limited. In recent years, Eritrea has made some efforts to engage with the international community. The government reversed an earlier decision to close U.N. operations and has allowed some nongovernmental organizations to return.

Earlier this year, they released four of a larger group of Djiboutian prisoners of war who were reunited with their families for the first time since 2008.

Eritrea has recently been more open to working with the European Union on development programs and has allowed a handful of international journalists to return to the country.

Eritrea's efforts to engage with the Office of High Commissioner for Human Rights are also welcome. The country accepted nearly half of the Universal Periodic Review recommendations and we continue to encourage the government to follow through on these.

But as I've noted, our bilateral relationship with Eritrea is not an easy one. But we have not and we do not seek to cut off diplomatic engagement nor communications. This summer, one of our Deputy Assistant Secretaries traveled to Asmara to visit our Embassy there.

Our Charge d'Affairs and her team meet regularly with officials and they host a variety of events at the American Center in Asmara for the Eritrean people.

Many challenges remain, yet I have to say I am impressed by the resiliency of the Eritrean people. Eritrea and Eritreans pride themselves in self-reliance in the face of adversity.

The largest obstacles to peace and prosperity, however, in their country have been erected by their own government.

We are encouraged by the small steps toward progress I have outlined above and we would urge the government to take much larger strides forward by ending indefinite national service and releasing political prisoners.

If given the opportunity to be heard and to fully and freely participate in their government, I truly believe that the people of Eritrea can do great things for their country.

We look forward to the day when that is possible.

Thank you very much for the opportunity to speak to you today and I look forward to your questions and if I can't answer I will turn to my colleague seated next to me.

[The prepared statement of Ambassador Thomas-Greenfield follows:]

**Testimony of
Assistant Secretary Linda Thomas-Greenfield
Bureau of African Affairs
before the
House of Representatives Committee on Foreign Affairs,
Subcommittee on Africa, Global Health, Global Human Rights, and
International Organizations
September 14, 2016**

Chairman Smith, Ranking Member Bass, and distinguished Members of the Committee, thank you for the opportunity to testify on the situation in Eritrea.

After twenty-five years of independence, Eritrea today stands as a country best known for its emigration and its poor record on human rights. Out of a population of approximately three million people, per UN estimates, an estimated five thousand people a month flee the country. Many risk a perilous journey across Africa and across the Mediterranean at the hands of sometimes ruthless smugglers and in unsafe vessels. The country is hemorrhaging its youth. In a country that has never known an election, Eritreans are voting with their feet. They are fleeing indefinite conscription into military or national service; religious persecution and other human rights violations; and economic hardship. These same conditions frame the United States' relationship with Eritrea.

In virtually every other country in Africa, including those with whom we have profound disagreements, we still seek to achieve partnerships across a range of shared global interests. We provide billions in foreign assistance to support those partnerships formed to fight HIV/AIDS and malaria; to support education; to combat violent extremism; and to strengthen governance. In Eritrea that is not the case and that is because of the decisions of the Eritrean government. In 2005, the Eritrean government ordered USAID, other donors, and international NGOs to leave the country. It subsequently ordered the Embassy's Defense Attaché office to close. As a result, we have no bilateral assistance, no military to military relationship, and—since 2010—no ambassador in Asmara.

This is not the relationship we desire. Eritrea is one of the poorest countries on Earth. It is located in a volatile and strategic neighborhood on the Red Sea. But if Eritrea likes to portray itself as David and the United States as Goliath, I would argue that its wounds are largely self-inflicted and its sling shot hurls stones at its own people. Up to five thousand of them make this clear every month, risking their lives rather than remaining in the country.

Eritrea's continuing torrent of emigration is no doubt driven in part by economic conditions, but it is its human rights record that pushes so many to leave. Over the past decade the Eritrean government has arbitrarily detained journalists, political opposition members, and others trying to express their opinions. In 2001, the Eritrean government detained without charge a group of reform-minded ministers and other prominent individuals who called for elections and implementation of the constitution. Many of these individuals remain imprisoned to this day. Almost all citizens, with few exceptions, are forced into indefinite conscription into national service and in many cases separated from their families for years. The Government has imposed severe restrictions on the exercise of freedom of religion and belief and has subjected members of "non-authorized" religions to arbitrary detention and forced recanting as a condition of release, as well as other ill-treatment. The Government has singled out groups such as the Jehovah's Witnesses for particularly harsh treatment because of their members' refusal to bear arms in the independence struggle or to participate in national service.

Eritrean officials have long justified their poor human rights record and large-scale militarization on an emergency "no war, no peace" situation over the unresolved demarcation of their border with Ethiopia. Eritrea has remained under a UN-imposed arms embargo and sanctions since 2009 for its actions that contributed to regional instability, including support for al-Shabaab in Somalia. In their last two annual reports, the UN's Somalia-Eritrea Monitoring Group has not found evidence of ongoing support to al-Shabaab, but Asmara's refusal to allow the group access to conduct investigations in Eritrea per its mandate, has limited the UN's ability to determine Eritrea's compliance with the sanctions regime. Eritrea also continues to hold Djiboutian prisoners of war and is accused of fomenting unrest in neighboring states.

For all these reasons, we have made it clear that turning a new page in the United States-Eritrea relationship first requires significant improvements in human rights. We have repeatedly called on the government to abide by its international human rights obligations, implement its own constitution, hold national elections, honor its commitment to limit the duration of national service to 18 months, develop an independent and transparent judiciary, and release persons who have been arbitrarily detained. We also continue to support the work of the Office of the UN High Commissioner for Human Rights, the UN Somalia-Eritrea Monitoring Group, and other international efforts to make progress.

And there has been some progress—albeit limited. In recent years, Eritrea has made some efforts to engage with the international community. The

Government reversed an earlier decision to close UN operations and has allowed some non-governmental organizations to return. Earlier this year they released four of the larger group of Djiboutian prisoners of war, who were reunited with their families for the first time since 2008. Eritrea has recently been more open to working with the European Union on development programs and has allowed a handful of international journalists to visit the country.

Eritrea's efforts to engage with the Office of the High Commissioner for Human Rights are also welcome. The country accepted nearly half of the Universal Periodic Review recommendations, and we continue to encourage the government to follow through on these.

As I have noted, our bilateral relationship with Eritrea is not easy, but we have not and do not seek to cut off diplomatic engagement and communication. This summer, one of our Deputy Assistant Secretaries traveled to Asmara to visit our embassy there. Our charge and her team meet regularly with officials and host a variety of events at the American Center in Asmara.

Many challenges remain. Yet I am impressed by the resiliency of the Eritrean people. Eritrea and Eritreans pride themselves on self-reliance in the face of adversity. The largest obstacles to peace and prosperity in their country have been erected by their own government. We are encouraged by the small steps towards progress I have outlined above. We would urge the government to take much larger strides forward by ending indefinite national service and releasing political prisoners. If given the opportunity to be heard and to fully and freely participate in their government, I believe that the people of Eritrea can do great things. We look forward to the day when that will be possible.

Thank you for providing me with the opportunity to speak today and I welcome any questions you may have.

_____

Mr. SMITH. Mr. Whitaker, I know you're on the spot a little bit but if you'd like to make some oral comments you're more than welcome.

Mr. WHITAKER. No, thank you, Mr. Chairman.

Mr. SMITH. Well, thank you. Then we'll move to some questions. First, beginning, if I could, with the Assistant Secretary. In your testimony you talk about Eritrea's efforts to engage the Office of High Commissioner for Human Rights are welcome, that the country has accepted nearly half of the Universal Periodic Review recommendations.

Could you elaborate on what they have agreed to and what remains focused upon and unaccomplished?

Ambassador THOMAS-GREENFIELD. It's a pretty long list. Eric, do you have the details of what they have agreed to? And if not, I will get back to you with that.

[The information referred to follows:]

WRITTEN RESPONSE RECEIVED FROM THE HONORABLE LINDA THOMAS-GREENFIELD TO QUESTION ASKED DURING THE HEARING BY THE HONORABLE CHRISTOPHER H. SMITH

A full list of the 200 Universal Periodic Review recommendations and the approximately half that were accepted can be found in the 2014 Report of the Working Group on the Universal Periodic Review for Eritrea and its addendum. Eritrea largely agreed to and prioritizes addressing the recommendations on health, education, poverty eradication and development, and women's rights. Eritrea also accepted recommendations to accede to certain international human rights conventions, such as the Convention Against Torture. Despite this, we note with concern continued allegations of torture in Eritrea and urge them to address this. We also regret that other conventions agreed to have not yet been ratified, such as the Worst Forms of Child Labor Convention.

Mr. WHITAKER. We can follow up with that in writing to be more specific, sir, but several areas in development, most notably in the sectors of health and education, greater transparency, allowing a larger number of visitors to obtain visas and to come and talk with government officials.

Mr. SMITH. Okay. If you could get back with a very detailed description of that, that would be very helpful. I met with the High Commissioner for Human Rights in New York for lunch several weeks ago. We talked about South Sudan. We talked about Eritrea and other hot spots that he is working on and expressing concerns about, Ethiopia as well.

Prince Zeid is doing his level best dealing with cauldrons all over the world, but if the council did agree that some progress was being made it would be helpful for this subcommittee to have that. So thank you.

Let me ask you with regards to former U.S. Ambassador to Eritrea, Ronald McMullen, who said that there were more than four dozen employees of the U.S. Embassy in Eritrea who were detained during his tenure.

Also, the daughter of the former Eritrean Minister of Information, Ciham Ali Abdu, who is also an American citizen is in prison. What can and are we doing to try to help her, to help others that either worked for us or are, in her case, an American and how many Americans are in Eritrean prisons?

Ambassador THOMAS-GREENFIELD. As far as I know, she is the only American who is currently in prison. We have had over the years our FSNs harassed—our Foreign Service National employees harassed, some arrested and some who are still currently being held by the government.

We never miss an opportunity to raise this with the Government of Eritrea, encouraging them to release the American citizen but also to release our employees who have been arrested and to discontinue the harassment of our employees.

Mr. SMITH. When we are in-country does the Embassy make active representations on their behalf? Do we get to visit? Are we just unaware of their fate?

Ambassador THOMAS-GREENFIELD. I'll let our former Charge d'Affairs answer that question.

Mr. WHITAKER. Yes, sir, I did make representations last month with the Ministry of Foreign Affairs in person verbally and in writing to Ciham. We've asked for consular access repeatedly and not been granted it. We are concerned regarding the case. The answers we get are typically vague or note that such individual is an Eritrean citizen.

Mr. SMITH. Do we know where she is? Do we have any kind of information about her health, the treatment or lack of good treatment for her?

Mr. WHITAKER. No, sir. We have not received specific responses to our questions, sir.

Mr. SMITH. Okay. Does her family know? Do they feed into our information based on her?

Mr. WHITAKER. I am not certain when their last communication with her was, sir.

Mr. SMITH. Okay. Let me ask you with regards to Father Habtu Ghebre-Ab has said that the government confiscates Bibles, punishes people for open prayer and, of course, Eritrea is a Country of Particular Concern and I am wondering what kind of impact the Office of International Religious Freedom has had.

Rabbi Saperstein, I know, is doing a wonderful job. Again, he has a full portfolio of egregious violators of religious freedom worldwide but this is a very serious issue and Father also makes a point in his testimony that national service is a form of human bondage and the TIP Report certainly goes into depth on that.

And then Dr. Khaled Beshir, who will be testifying, points out that there may be as many 20,000 eleventh graders who have been forced to work for the ruling party, supplying workers for Nevsun. He describes it as slave labor.

Do we have any information on that? It would appear like the parallel child soldiering issue, forced labor of very young children and teenagers and, again, it is in the narrative again this year of our TIP Report.

But what can we do to help on this? Has UNICEF engaged, because they are leaders when it comes to the exploitation of children.

Ambassador THOMAS-GREENFIELD. Certainly, you noted and we noted as well that on the religious freedom scale Eritrea is a Country of Particular Concern and that the freedom to practice religion is strongly restricted by the government even for those three or four religions that they recognize.

And this is an important issue for us and we've reflected that in our International Religious Freedom Report and it is an issue that we do as well continue to raise with the government.

On the issue of national service, one of the things that the Eritrean Government agreed to was that they would limit, in the future, national service to 18 months.

They have not honored that commitment and for now national service is almost for life, and what that means is that these young people are not able to take care of their families.

They're not able to even plan for their futures. They are basically in a form of bondage for the rest of their lives. At eleventh grade they go into training and they are divided up and sent to various locations where they are required to perform their national service.

Again, Eric was on the ground and may be able to provide a little more detail on that.

Mr. WHITAKER. Thank you, ma'am.

Yes, Mr. Chairman. With respect to the national service after completion of eleventh grade, as she had said, students proceed to the Sawa training camp.

They basically are divided into three groups thereafter. A small portion continue to higher education. A certain number go into military service on behalf of the security services of the country and the largest group goes into community service wherein they may be assigned to the various ministries or other parastatals or other branches of the government.

But this is where the youth of the country goes and the service is indeterminate in length and this is one of the reasons that the youth are departing the country.

Mr. SMITH. Just a few final questions, then I'll yield to Ranking Member Bass. Can you describe why the government is showing some interest in reaching out to the international community, particularly some of these NGOs and providers of humanitarian aid in the E.U.?

What's behind this motivation? What steps would need to be taken for the United States to upgrade its diplomatic standing? Is there any movement in that? Do you sense a positive or a movement in that regard?

The Ethiopian and Eritrean forces clashed along the border of the Tsorona area. In his testimony, Dr. Beshir points out that resolution of the Eritrea-Ethiopia border dispute would take Eritrea out of its war footing, which is its justification for universal national service.

What is your sense of that? What is being done to try to make that work? And finally, when an Eritrean man or woman goes to sea or goes to flight into Sudan, for example, or to Europe or wherever, if they are brought back what is the penalty that they suffer as a result of this attempted flight for refugee status?

Ambassador THOMAS-GREENFIELD. The first question was, why do we think the Eritrean Government continues or is opening up for opportunities to engage with the international community? And I think the answer to that is really simple and that is the sanctions have increased the cost of Eritrea's policies.

So they need the development assistance that the European Union and NGOs might be able to provide for them, particularly in the health and education sector where they are allowing the few NGOs that they have allowed to come back in—the kind of work that they are allowing them to do.

So I think their motive is a simple one. Their motive is simply need and as this effort continues we've not really seen any positive changes on the part of the government in terms of those areas that are important for us to change the nature of our engagement with the government.

Those issues really require that the government take some serious measures to deal with the human rights situation in the country, to deal with the issues of press freedom, to deal with the issues of freedom of religion, to change their policy on national service, to limit it to 18 months so that these young people are able to engage in livelihoods that will allow them to have a future in the country.

On the Ethiopia-Eritrea border dispute, we have encouraged both sides to work on a path to address this dispute.

The report from the U.N. was I think very clear and we hope that both sides look for ways other than through conflict, through war, to address this.

I don't know exactly what the penalty is if someone is returned. I suspect it is not a good thing for them and I would suspect that they would be either arrested or forced to continue their national service.

Mr. SMITH. If you could get back to us on that, yes, it would be helpful.

WRITTEN RESPONSE RECEIVED FROM THE HONORABLE LINDA THOMAS-GREENFIELD TO QUESTION ASKED DURING THE HEARING BY THE HONORABLE CHRISTOPHER H. SMITH

According to our Country Report on Human Rights Practices for 2015, in general Eritreans had the right to return to Eritrea, but citizens residing abroad had to show proof they paid the two percent tax on foreign earned income and sign a statement of regret. People known to have been declared ineligible for political asylum by other governments had their requests to reenter the country scrutinized more than others. Many who fled Eritrea remain in self-imposed exile due to fears that they would be conscripted into national service or detained for their beliefs if they returned. In some cases, security forces reportedly have arrested, detained, tortured, and beaten national service and military deserters and evaders and other people attempting to flee the country without travel documents.

However, other sources reported there were little to no consequences for returning Eritreans, particularly those who had been granted residency or citizenship in other countries. Given the limited access within Eritrea, our Embassy has not been able to verify reported treatment of returnees.

Ambassador THOMAS-GREENFIELD. Eric, do you know?

Mr. WHITAKER. Mr. Chairman, I was going to follow on the development side.

The first question, foremost, during my recent stay in Asmara as Charge d'Affairs at our Embassy I spent quite a bit of time talking to U.N. agency heads and their other representatives and my counterparts with the other Embassies.

The door is slowly opening for development cooperation but I pick my words carefully—it is development cooperation for the long term in close coordination with ministries as opposed to short-term humanitarian assistance. The government is very adamant about this.

The sectors which are allowed the most entry by outside partners—development partners—are in the health and education sectors. So the door is slowly opening.

A limited number of NGOs—JICA from Japan, the U.N. agencies, and the E.U. development fund, as you mentioned earlier. These are all carefully negotiated agreements. This door is slowly opening.

The number that flees each month doesn't seem to be slowing down. It's 5,000 a month. The UNHCR told us that very directly by the registration of those departing the country, arriving elsewhere.

But I am not aware of circumstances of those who were forcibly returned. That's not come to my attention.

Thank you, sir.

Mr. SMITH. Thank you very much.

I yield to Ms. Bass.

Ms. BASS. Thank you. Thank you very much for your testimony and I especially want to thank Mr. Whitaker, knowing we put you on the spot there but really appreciate your input.

Eritrea remains such a mystery and I wanted to know if you could describe a little bit about what life is like there and also what is the ideology of the regime? What is driving it? You described the national service. You described it in three different categories—higher ed, the military and government service. What determines which way one goes?

That's to begin.

Mr. WHITAKER. Thank you for that question, Madam Ranking Member. The problem is when one is in Asmara one sees only a limited spectrum of society of Eritrea. Our ability to travel, rather, in country is somewhat limited.

Most Eritreans are engaged in small-scale agriculture—herding, millet, sorghum, other crops. Their life is relatively simple. In urban areas it is more limited. Many of the people we are encountering are working with parastatals.

Ms. BASS. What?

Mr. WHITAKER. Are working at the parastatals, state-owned enterprises——

Ms. BASS. Oh.

Mr. WHITAKER [continuing]. And small-scale businesses or perhaps working with the NGOs or Embassies. Many folks, of course, are in community service including many of the employees at the government ministries.

We see in the economy that the mining sector and the remittances sent by those abroad are very important to keeping the economy going.

I think the fact that 5,000 people are leaving a month is a reflection in part not just on human rights but also diminished life chances and that is that many don't seem many economic opportunities so they decide that perhaps it is better to take their chances to depart the country and send back remittances to support their relatives.

Ms. BASS. You described the inability to travel very much and so why is that? Does the government—you know, we have the—we have that relationship, like, with Cuba, for example.

You know, U.S. diplomats and Cuban diplomats couldn't travel beyond a 25-mile radius. What is limiting their movement in Asmara?

Mr. WHITAKER. The current limitation is on all internationals in Asmara. They must apply with the Ministry of Foreign Affairs in advance in writing to depart from a 25-mile radius of Asmara.

Ms. BASS. Okay. So I am still trying to——

Ambassador THOMAS-GREENFIELD. Excuse me, we have that same policy for Eritrean diplomats here in the United States as well.

Ms. BASS. I see. So I am——

Ambassador THOMAS-GREENFIELD. It's reciprocal.

Ms. BASS [continuing]. Still trying to understand the society so that is why I asked what is the ideology that is driving this. Is this a socialist regime? It reminds me of Cambodia, in Cambodia people were forced from the city to the rural areas. So what is the underlying ideology of the government that leads the country to be organized this way?

Ambassador THOMAS-GREENFIELD. I would argue that it is an ideology that is based on a strong sense of sovereignty and independence and self-reliance that came out of the many years of fighting and their independence movement and they are still a lot of people who strongly believe in that ideology and are willing to deal with the extensive adversity that people are under there to continue to survive.

But I do think that it is time for change and I think most Eritreans believe that it is time for change and they deserve a peaceful transition.

Ms. BASS. Do they see themselves as a socialist country? I know that there is very limited private sector so is that how they see themselves?

Ambassador THOMAS-GREENFIELD. I have not heard that terminology used. I've heard self-reliance more used as a philosophy.

Ms. BASS. So what determines then in the three categories—higher education, community service, and military? Community service doesn't sound bad so tell me why it is.

Ambassador THOMAS-GREENFIELD. They use this to ensure that they have the people to do the various activities that they require of their people. So I was told recently that you see large numbers of people who are in government service who are directing traffic outside, for example.

Ms. BASS. Do they not get paid?

Ambassador THOMAS-GREENFIELD. I think it is a very limited amount.

Mr. WHITAKER. Yes, ma'am. It is a low pay. We've heard as low as $10 a month.

Ms. BASS. Do they have parts of their lives subsidized? Is housing subsidized? Do they have a healthcare system? I mean, how do they function?

Ambassador THOMAS-GREENFIELD. I'd be interested in hearing our Eritrean colleagues, who are coming next. But I know that——

Ms. BASS. Oh, okay.

Ambassador THOMAS-GREENFIELD [continuing]. A huge part of how they function is through their family members who are living elsewhere——

Ms. BASS. Remittances.

Ambassador THOMAS-GREENFIELD [continuing]. The diaspora community supporting families.

Ms. BASS. So, once again, what determines higher education, government service, and military?

Ambassador THOMAS-GREENFIELD. I think we are going to have to get back. Those are the three categories they use and I am not sure how they decide——

Ms. BASS. Who goes where.

Ambassador THOMAS-GREENFIELD [continuing]. Who goes where.

Ms. BASS. Okay.

[The information referred to follows:]

WRITTEN RESPONSE RECEIVED FROM MR. ERIC WHITAKER TO QUESTION ASKED
DURING THE HEARING BY THE HONORABLE KAREN BASS

By law all Eritrean citizens between ages 18 and 50 must perform national service, with limited exceptions. The national service obligation essentially begins after the final year of secondary school at Sawa National Service Training Center. Good marks on the final exams are required to be assigned to one of the seven government colleges. Those who do not receive high enough grades are immediately assigned to military or national service. National service in theory consists of six months of military training and 12 months of active military service and development tasks in the military forces for a total of 18 months. However, as we've noted, the period of service in practice is indefinite in nature. For those unfit to undergo military training, they may be assigned to a public and government organ according to their capacity and reportedly perform standard patrols and border monitoring in addition to labor such as agricultural terracing, planting, road maintenance, hotel work, teaching, construction, and laying power lines. An Amnesty International Report on national service called "Just Deserters" also found that "conscripts collected through round-ups rather than through school are more frequently sent to military training camps than other areas of national service."

Ambassador THOMAS-GREENFIELD. I think most people want to go to higher education——

Ms. BASS. Yes.

Ambassador THOMAS-GREENFIELD [continuing]. Because it is not a——

Ms. BASS. But then, okay, so you go to higher education and what can you do with it?

Ambassador THOMAS-GREENFIELD. You teach, you work in schools, you do whatever the government wants you to do in the education sector.

Ms. BASS. And—oh, and so I am assuming that these three categories are both men and women. So are women in the military?

Ambassador THOMAS-GREENFIELD. Women are in the military and Eritrean women were known for their activities and their abilities during the fight for independence.

Ms. BASS. So what is the rationale of the E.U. then in terms of the developmental assistance because you too said, I believe, we provide no developmental assistance but the E.U. does.

Ambassador THOMAS-GREENFIELD. It's simple and it just started. It's because they are the largest beneficiary of these 5,000 people a month who are fleeing the country.

Ms. BASS. Oh, they want them to stay there. Right.

Ambassador THOMAS-GREENFIELD. They are looking for development opportunities so people don't leave.

Ms. BASS. Do you know how they do development assistance, meaning are there European NGOs that actually get the money versus the Eritrean people?

We fund NGOs a lot of times, right? Our own NGOs.

Mr. WHITAKER. Yes, ma'am. The E.U. Development Fund does provide funding through specific ministries, especially in health and education. JICA is there, the Japanese International Cooperation Agency.

The NGOs include Finn Church Aid, the Norwegian Refugee Council, Vita from Ireland and they provide services predominantly in health and education sectors as well.

Ms. BASS. Do you think we should start providing assistance?

Ambassador THOMAS-GREENFIELD. I don't think we've reached the point where we can provide assistance to this government. We are looking for certain changes to occur in how the government functions, how the government operates and how it treats its people. So at the moment there are no plans for us to provide for their assistance.

Ms. BASS. Are people still trying to flee to Israel?

Mr. WHITAKER. Ma'am, I don't believe so. The pattern that I have noted, and this is in discussion with UNHCR and quite a number of others including ICRC, is that most refugees depart for Ethiopia or Sudan, finding their way up through Egypt and Libya, going across the Mediterranean often to join relatives that are in Italy, the U.K., Switzerland or elsewhere within Europe.

Ms. BASS. Thank you very much.

I yield back.

Mr. SMITH. Just let me ask one final question, if I could. In her testimony, Ms. Bruton, deputy director of the Africa Center at the Atlantic Council, points out that what so far is missing from the record is Eritrean Government's point of view.

She testifies that the absence of this perspective is terribly dangerous to U.S. interests in the Horn of Africa and beyond and it is painfully, then, easy to get it wrong.

Obviously, with Mr. Whitaker here who has been in-country and was our representative there as Charge d'Affairs, and Ambassador Thomas-Greenfield, your work with the entire backing of a State Department that works very hard to get it right, have we misperceived Eritrea somehow?

It seems to me that when it comes to fundamental human rights and as you both have said people voting with their feet because of a serious wave of repression and poverty, self-isolation of shooting one's self in the foot, when people raise the issue of adjacent Ethiopia—both Greg and I were in Ethiopia in 2005 and met with President Meles and on the plane began sketching out the Ethiopian Human Rights Act because so many dissenters were shot in the streets.

And yesterday we introduced H. Res. 861 and are planning a series of hearings on Ethiopia to very strongly protest the gross violations of human rights, the murders that are taking place.

At our press conference yesterday we had the silver medalist for the marathon who spoke very effectively about this attack on Ethiopia.

And so this subcommittee takes a back seat to no one in trying to be as clearheaded and focused on human rights abuses wherever and, of course, the country, on human rights practices, is a textbook on these abuses, and I thank you for that. Again, the CPC designation couldn't be more clear and the Tier 3 designation in the TIP Report couldn't be more clear as well.

So are we somehow getting it wrong, as Ms. Bruton suggests?

Ambassador THOMAS-GREENFIELD. Sir, I think the facts on the ground in Eritrea speak for themselves. We are dealing with a situation where we do have strong evidence of violation of human rights in Eritrea.

But that said, it is important that we engage this government and we do engage the government. We have diplomatic relations with the Government of Eritrea and so we do engage with this government, both through our Embassy in Asmara as well as through our contacts with the Charge d'Affairs here and when they've had government officials come to the country and I encourage the Eritrean Government to engage.

If they have a story to tell, if they want us to understand the situation better, the Somalia-Eritrea Monitoring Group should be allowed to come in and should be allowed to engage so that they can tell their side of the story so that if we are not getting it right we can see the evidence of that.

But right now, the evidence that we have point to the fact that serious human rights conditions exist in this country and that we need to continue to address those until we see that they no longer exist.

Mr. SMITH. And Mr. Whitaker, thank you so much for your testimony. If you could get back with some of those answers to elaborate and we might have some additional questions that will be posed to you, we would deeply appreciate it.

I'd like to now welcome our second panel, beginning with Father Habtu Ghebre-Ab. He serves as a parish priest in Holy Trinity Eritrean Orthodox Church in Cincinnati, Ohio.

He is also the director of external relations for the Canonical Eritrean Orthodox Church in Diaspora under the imprisoned Patriarch and His Holiness' designated bishop. The Diaspora Diocese includes all of North America, Europe, and the Middle East.

He is a senior faculty member with a rank of full professor at the University of Cincinnati where he has taught for over a quarter of a century. The focus of his study is African history, specializing in colonial history in the Horn of Africa.

For several years now he has published several articles on and advocating for religious freedom, separation of church and state and on behalf of all political prisoners in Eritrea.

Secondly, we'll hear from Dr. Khaled Beshir, who is a board member of the Awate Foundation, a world media service on Eritrea which promotes peace and reconciliation within Eritrea. He is an independent risk management consultant and subject matter expert in the Horn of Africa, specializing in development finance.

He advises various U.N. agencies, international organizations, investors, and law firms on assessment of geopolitical, regulatory, and financial risks. As an Eritrean-American and longtime advocate of human rights in Eritrea for the last 25 years, he works closely with Eritrean civil societies, political organizations, media outlets, and community leaders.

In 2000, he was a member of a group of Eritrean intellectuals and professionals who met with the Eritrean President and urged him to introduce political and economic reform and respect for the rule of law.

And third, we will hear from Ms. Bruton, who is deputy director of the Atlantic Council's Africa Center. She is a recognized authority on the Horn of Africa. She is especially well-known for authoring a series of prominent reports and journal essays on Somalia. She provides regular expert commentary on African political affairs for major international media and held an international affairs fellowship at the Council on Foreign Relations and the Center for Strategic and International Studies.

Prior to her fellowship appointment, Ms. Bruton managed the National Endowment for Democracy's multi-million dollar portfolio of small grants to local and international nongovernmental organizations operating in east and southern Africa and managed post-conflict political transition programs in Africa for the U.S. Agency for International Development.

She has also served as a policy analyst on international affairs and trade team for the Government Accountability Office.

So Father Habtu, if you could begin.

STATEMENT OF FATHER HABTU GHEBRE-AB, DIRECTOR OF EXTERNAL RELATIONS, CANONICAL ERITREAN ORTHODOX CHURCH IN DIASPORA

Father GHEBRE-AB. The Honorable Chairman Smith and members of the subcommittee, I thank you for the privilege of being here today to give my testimony on the challenges Eritrea represents and why failure to positively contribute to the resolutions of these challenges will affect the entire region and beyond.

My name is Father Athanasius Habtu Ghebre-Ab. I am an Eritrean-American, a professor of history at the University of Cincinnati and an ordained priest in the Eritrean Orthodox Church.

I am pained by the general instability in the Horn of Africa and the unresolved conflict and animus between Ethiopia and Eritrea, which, in one way or another, remains at the very root of the instability in the region.

We also note the untold and continuing suffering of the people of Eritrea and the dashing of the early optimism and hopes the world initially saw for this new country.

We have also witnessed the extreme reluctance of the United States, a country which the people of the region rightly or wrongly have historically looked to as a reliant mediating power.

In the remaining time I have, please allow me to speak to you about one aspect of Eritrea's egregious human rights violations, namely, its denial of religious freedom to its people, a subject of my expertise.

The following are but a few facts. Long before all the independent press in Eritrea were ruthlessly shot down in September 2001, the publications of the Eritrean Orthodox Church and the Roman Catholic Church were shut down.

In 1994, the Jehovah's Witnesses became the first victims. Within a month, the government unleashed massive campaigns of arrest and disappearance against the Muslim community in Eritrea.

Next, the government's systematic anti-religious campaign moved to the ranks of the military, especially in Sawa, the sprawling military training camp near the Sudanese border.

Here, all Bibles were confiscated and anyone caught praying was subjected to the cruelest treatments by the military establishment. This practice was soon expanded throughout the military across the country.

In April 2002, the government passed a sweeping decree closing all minority Christian denominations and other sects. Soon after, the leaders and adherents were vigorously rounded up and imprisoned and I personally witnessed that at the time.

The government accelerated the total control of the largest and most ancient religious institution in Eritrea, the Eritrean Orthodox Church.

In November 2004, the leading lights of the church were imprisoned. A little over a year later, the Patriarch of the Eritrean Orthodox Church, His Holiness Abune Antonis, was illegally deposed from his Patriarchal throne and imprisoned.

This was followed by the subsequent imprisonment of hundreds of other clergies. Today, it is estimated that between 2,000 to 3,000 people are in prison for their faith.

The question now is what is to be done to bring about stability to Eritrea and the region. The Eritrean Government should immediately implement the Constitution that was ratified in 1997 but was never implemented.

This will guarantee its people the rights enshrined therein, thus removing fear, uncertainty and the guarantees of rights.

The so-called national service has degenerated into an unsustainable, unjust and immoral practice which results in the youth fleeing the country in such a large number it must come to an immediate end.

The thousands of prisoners of conscience must be released. The United States should reengage with the Government of Ethiopia and Eritrea to end the so-called ''no war, no peace'' state of affairs for the past 16 years and mediate lasting peace in the region by helping in the implementation of the Ethiopian-Eritrean boundary commission ruling of April 13, 2002.

Eritrea and Ethiopia must be encouraged to cease hosting armed opposition groups in their respective countries to destabilize one another. Again, I thank you.

[The prepared statement of Father Ghebre-Ab follows:]

Fr. Athanasius Habtu Ghebre-Ab, Ph.D.
Director of External Relations,
The Canonical Diaspora Diocese of the Eritrean Orthodox Church
(North America, Europe and the Middle East)
September 14, 2016

COMMITTEE ON FOREIGN AFFAIRS
Subcommittee on Africa, Global Health, Global Human Rights, and International
Organizations

Eritrea: A Neglected Regional Threat

The Honorable Chairman Smith and members of the Subcommittee, I thank you for the privilege of being here today to give my testimony on the challenges Eritrea represents, and why failure to positively contribute in the resolutions of these challenges will affect the entire region and beyond.

My name is Fr. Athanasius Habtu Ghebre-Ab. I am an Eritrean-American and one who is deeply affected by events in Eritrea; a professor of history at the University of Cincinnati where I have taught for a quarter of a century; and also an ordained priest in the Eritrean Orthodox Church (ErOC). In the case of the latter, besides pastoring an Orthodox parish, I also serve as Director of External Relations for the Diaspora Dioceses of the ErOC in North America, Europe and the Middle East.

Although my own personal story is not and should not be the focus here, as I come before you to testify on the present situation in Eritrea, I believe that my multiple identity and life-experiences shed light on the fact that they substantially inform my views on the subject at hand. Because I was born in Ethiopia where I spent my formative years, I am deeply touched by my roots there. But because my parents were of Eritrean origin and the country remains hallowed to me and my family because of my two brothers who gave the ultimate sacrifice for its independence, Eritrea will always hold a special place in my heart as well. Finally, let me say that I have lived my entire adult life in the United States, my beloved adopted country, the country of my children and the country that has handed me all its promises opportunities. Therefore, as I have often said, I am a child of these great heritages. And I am blessed for it.

I say all of these to make the point that I am pained by the general instability in the Horn of Africa, the unresolved conflict and animus between Ethiopia and Eritrea, which, in one way or another, remains at the very root of the instability in the region. One also can trace the untold and continuing suffering of the people of Eritrea and the dashing of the early optimism and hopes the world initially saw for this new country to the same root cause. It also pains me to see that the United States, a country which the people of the region - rightly or wrongly - have historically looked to as a reliant mediating power and still holds a huge diplomatic sway has increasingly shown reluctance to reengage with them in order to contribute toward bringing about a lasting peace in the region.

Please allow me to refocus my testimony to the main subject today – Eritrea - a country whose leaders presently stand accused of "crimes against humanity" by the most recent report of the UN Commission of Inquiry on Eritrea.

Eritrea has of late achieved the dubious distinction as the "North Korea of Africa" for establishing the most repressive regime the people have ever experienced. It has stripped the people of any semblance of the most primordial rights and subjected them to innumerable indignities. The country has no parliament. It has refused to implement the only constitution that its people ratified in 1997, five years following its achievement of independence. Mr. Isayas Afeworki's government holds thousands of prisoners of conscience in its notorious prisons without so much as a semblance of trial. In fact, the country has no working judicial system to speak of. The government has closed all independent media and is known as a country that holds the largest numbers of journalist in prison as a ration of its population. Up to five to six thousand people, mostly the young, continue to flee the country each month for the past several years largely because of the policy the regime euphemistically refers to as "national service." This is the most unusual policy by any country in recent history, requiring its young people to serve in the military for indefinite period without a living wage. This practice has actually morphed itself into the sort of human bondage - slavery - by the regime in an unprecedented scale. Today, the country, small as it is with a population of perhaps only five million, yet produces one of the largest number of refugees in the world. We have all witnessed the tragic death of hundreds of men, women and children at a time in the Mediterranean Sea as they sailed in search of safe havens in Europe.

Please allow me now to speak to you about one aspect of Eritrea's egregious human rights violations, namely, its denial of religious freedom to its people, a subject of my expertise. And one point that needs to be emphasized here is that no faith community in Eritrea is spared the enmity and extremely heavy-handed treatment by the government. The following are but a few examples.

- Long before all the independent press in Eritrea were ruthlessly shut down in September 2001, *Fnote Brhan* and *Hiwet,* the main publications (organs) of the Eritrean Orthodox Church (ErOC) and the Roman Catholic Church, respectively, were already ordered closed.
- In 1994, the Jehovah's Witnesses became the first victims. They were rendered an illegal sect. Their citizenship rights were revoked, and were soon rounded up and imprisoned.
- Within a month, the government unleashed another massive campaign of arrest and disappearance against the Muslim community in Eritrea.
- Next, the government's systematic anti-religious campaign moved to the ranks of the military, especially in Sawa, the sprawling military training camp near the Sudanese border. Here, all bibles were confiscated and anyone caught praying was subjected to the cruelest treatments by the military establishment. This practice was soon expanded throughout the military across the country.
- In April 2002 the government passed a sweeping decree closing all minority Christian denominations and other sects. Soon after, their leaders and adherents were vigorously rounded up and imprisoned. I happened to be in Eritrea at the time and witnessed the terror.
- The government accelerated the total control of the largest and most ancient religious institution in Eritrea – the ErOC. In November 2004 the leading lights of the Church were imprisoned. The Reverend Dr. Fitsum Ghebrenegus, a priest and renown psychiatrist, the Reverend Dr. Tecle-Ab Mengste-Ab, a priest and a highly respected physician, *Merigeta* Yitbarek Berhe, a leading priest and a scholar, Fr. Ghebremedhin Ghebre-Giorgis, a well-known figure in the ErOC and countless others were rounded up and imprisoned. They have never been charged with any crime as they languish in prison for the past twelve years, as do hundreds of other priests and monks. A little over a year later, the Patriarch

of the ErOC, H.H. Abune Antonios, was illegally deposed from his patriarchal throne and imprisoned. His only crimes were that he insisted that the government desist from interference in the affairs of the Church and calling for the release of prisoners of conscience. Although ninety-years of age now, he remains *incommunicado*. This was followed by the subsequent imprisonment of hundreds of clergies. With these and many other acts, the ErOC has been totally taken over by the government. Its every act are controlled by the Religious Affairs Department, an agency of the government, and those that represent its interests.

Today, it is estimated that between 2,000-3,000 people are in prison in Eritrea for their faith. The condition of their incarceration is as harsh as the thousands of other prisoners of conscience throughout Eritrea. Owing to this sustained denial of religious freedom in Eritrea, the US Commission for International Religious Freedom has consistently designated the country as one of the few "Countries of Particular Concern."

At this critical juncture, the question that one must ask, therefore, is what is to be done to bring about stability to Eritrea and the region.

(1) The Eritrean Government should immediately implement the constitutions that was ratified in 1997, but was never implemented. This will guarantee its people the rights enshrined therein, thus removing fear, uncertainty and the guarantees of rights.

(2) The so-called "national service" might have initially been brought about by one's historical experiences, and the imagined or real fear and suspicion of the intentions of others. But because the practice has degenerated into an unsustainable, unjust and immoral practice which results in the youth fleeing the country in such a huge number, it must come to an immediate end.

(3) The thousands of prisoners of conscience must be released.

(4) The United States should re-engage with the governments of Ethiopia and Eritrea to end the so-called "No-War-No-Peace" state of affairs of the past sixteen years and bring a lasting peace in the region by helping in the implementation of the Ethiopia-Eritrea Boundary Commission ruling of April 13, 2002.

(5) Eritrea and Ethiopia must be encouraged to cease hosting armed opposition groups in their respective countries to destabilize the other.

I ask you to take up the cause of a people, who, although so far away geographically from us, are nevertheless linked to us by their universal yearning: to breathe the air of freedom.

I thank you for this opportunity.

Mr. SMITH. Thank you so very much for your testimony and for your concrete recommendations to the subcommittee and by extension to the White House and the State Department. Thank you so much.

I'd like to now ask Dr. Beshir if you would proceed.

STATEMENT OF KHALED BESHIR, PH.D., BOARD MEMBER, AWATE FOUNDATION

Mr. BESHIR. Thank you, Mr. Chairman, Ranking Member Bass for giving me this opportunity to testify in this important hearing to evaluate the U.S. policy toward Eritrea. My name is Khaled Beshir. I am a long time advocate of human rights in Eritrea.

My testimony will be shaped by 25 years of closely following the activities of the Government of Eritrea, those who are still in power and those who were once in power who have been exiled or made to disappear, and I presume in jail or dead.

In this hearing, I will try to, as I outline it in my written statement, say why the unconditional engagement of Eritrea as recommended by some is dangerous and a short answer to that it has been tried before.

To start with, the reason the Eritrean regime is as bad as it is, topping the list of every human rights organizations is precisely because for 8 long years the United States and Western Europe gave it unconditional support.

This was between 1991 and 1998. When the new government was given the benefit of the doubt, the Clinton administration provided military assistance, facilitated low interest loans and grants, and contributed in capacity building and praised the autocratic system routinely, calling it part of the Africa Renaissance, a short-lived description praising the heads of state of Ethiopia, Uganda, Rwanda, Congo, and Eritrea.

And what was the outcome? Ethiopia is what you see in the headlines today. The leaders of Uganda and Rwanda amended their Constitutions to extend their rule. Congo descended into civil war. And it is during that period of unconditional engagement that all these atrocities in Eritrea the Eritrean regime is infamous for—arbitrary arrest, disappearance, banning religious organizations, exiling, severe restriction on civil liberties—were germinated.

So for those who are arguing that there should be unconditional resumption of U.S.-Eritrean relations all they need to look is back at the history of the early 1990s and this is why we are here.

As far as the human rights conditions are concerned, it has been extensively covered by the U.N. Special Rapporteur on the situation of human rights in Eritrea and the Commission of Inquiry on Human Rights in Eritrea.

So rather than speaking about the human rights violations in Eritrea—it has been extensively documented—I would like to speak about—very little known about the role of Nevsun, the Canadian mining company that has finally disclosed that it has been funding the Atlantic Council campaign for the last 18 months to rehabilitate the image of Eritrea and whitewash the human rights abuses and calling for the unconditional U.S. engagement in Eritrea.

The reason is the interest of Nevsun, the mining company, is intertwined with the interests of the regime. Nevsun Resource is a Canadian mining company and the Eritrean Government, through ENAMCO, jointly owned the Bisha Mine. That's the only source—revenue-generating source for Nevsun.

Why, you might ask why, would that be important for Nevsun? Aside that it has been accused of militarizing commerce and using slave labor in building the Bisha Mine is for the following reason.

Simply, in the last 5 years the stock valuation in Nevsun has stagnated at about $3.50 for the last 6 years. This is unusually very low for a company that sits at $1.3 billion of assets.

So Nevsun tried many things to improve this image. It sold and failed to be acquired by a larger firm. It failed to diversify its single source of revenue from Bisha. It failed to impress investors and shareholders by glossy and unaudited corporate responsibility and environmental reports.

It has failed to shake off its reputation as an enabler of human rights-abusing regimes. It has failed the human rights organizations that it no longer uses slave labor. It failed to comply with the United Nations Somalia-Eritrean Monitoring Group's request to disclose financial transactions records.

Simply, it has failed to bring any meaningful economic betterment to the lives of Eritreans other than enriching the coffers of the regime.

So Nevsun thought to rehabilitate its image instead. Knowing that its efforts were hampered by Eritrea's dismal human record, Nevsun quickly settled multiple lawsuits, paying close to $30 million, hired a public relations firm, hired a purported human rights attorney, and courted the diplomatic community in Asmara.

Still, all its efforts failed. While overt attempts failed to make a dent, Nevsun turned to a more subtle approach to funding the Atlantic Council to rehabilitate its image and that of Eritrea so that it can lobby on its behalf.

We often see the vice president of Nevsun and one of the associates of the Atlantic Council, Ms. Bruton, appearing in the ruling party's events and rallies and speaking to drum up support for the regime.

So in short, to conclude my statement, I would like to say that Eritrea is mineral-rich country. It's strategically located in the Horn of Africa and the Red Sea where the U.S. has vital strategic interests and legitimate concern in its ongoing counterterrorism campaign.

Hence, the U.S.' strategic interest should not depend on the fate of one ailing man, particularly when dealing with a regime that not only does not share any of the values of the U.S. enshrined but routinely mocks it.

While recognizing that the Eritrean people's challenge could only be resolved by Eritreans, it is prudent for the U.S. to be prepared to deal not with how to rehabilitate President Isaias' image, who has no support by Eritreans and rules by fear, but with the post-Eritrea by taking the following steps aimed at shortening the suffering of the Eritrean people and safeguarding U.S. interests in the region and they are as follows: To deny President Isaias the excuse to maintain a war footing, pressure Ethiopia to allow the demarcation of the border and to proceed at least in the 95 percent of the undisputed borders area, continue making human rights issues a precondition for U.S.-Eritrea relations, continue supporting the current U.N.-sponsored sanctions against Eritrea until the conditions for lifting are met, support the U.N. Security Council members' initiative to refer the U.N. Human Rights Commission of Inquiry to the International Criminal Court, provide humanitarian assistance to Eritrean refugees and to provide immigrant visas to help them come to the U.S. and ask other countries to do so, especially of the unaccompanied minors that are fleeing Eritrea now and Ethiopian—in the refugee camps in Ethiopia. Also provide temporary protective status for Eritrean refugees who are already in the U.S., to support regional organization government efforts in combating human trafficking in the Horn of Africa but also, most importantly, I urge you to sanction mining companies like Nevsun that are engaged in militarized commerce and using conscripted labor force by designating their production as conflict minerals.

People who suffer under totalitarian regimes look up to the world community, especially the United States, for support. They become disappointed and disillusioned when they discovered misinformed consultants in a position to advise government.

It is disheartening to see aggressive approaches to absolving a totalitarian regime, the individuals who have no personal stake in the outcome and only interested to promote their careers and personal interest.

The liberal democratic force in Eritrea has a great potential to grow but attempts to bury it in its infancy by using the ''there is no viable opposition'' claim is a crime against the Eritrean people.

I urge this august body not to repeat the mistakes committed during the Clinton era when the Eritrean dictator was hailed as a renaissance leader and provided with all the source of support, a lifeline that had helped it grow into the monster that it has become.

I urge this body to take the right decision, a decision inspired by American values. I urge you to remain a beacon of hope for the young democratic force, inspire them with the right decision, with the much-wronged Eritrean citizens in mind.

Thank you, and I look forward to your questions.

[The prepared statement of Mr. Beshir follows:]

Testimony of Khaled Beshir, Ph.D.
Board Member, Awate Foundation

Wednesday, September 14, 2016 at 2:00 PM

Hearing before the House Committee on foreign Affairs,
Subcommittee on Africa, Global Health, Global Human
Rights, and International Organizations

"Eritrea: A Neglected Regional Threat"

Thank you Mr. Chairman, Ranking Member Bass, and Members of the Subcommittee for giving me this opportunity to testify at this important hearing to evaluate US policy towards Eritrea.

I am an independent risk management consultant and a subject matter expert in the Horn of Africa specializing in development finance. I advise various UN agencies, international organizations, investors, and law firms on assessment of geopolitical, regulatory, and financial risks. As an Eritrean-American and a longtime advocate of human rights in Eritrea (for the last twenty five years), I work closely with Eritrean civil societies, political organizations, media outlets, and community leaders. In 2000, I was a member of a group of Eritrean intellectuals and professionals (known as G-13) who met President Isaias Afeworki and urged him to introduce political and economic reform and to respect the rule of law. I am a board member of Awate Foundation, an Eritrean platform for information dissemination, opinion sharing and promoting peace and reconciliation.

My testimony is shaped by 25 years of closely following the activities of the Government of Eritrea--those still in power, and the once-powerful who have been exiled or made to disappear and are presumed jailed or dead--rather than 18 months of discovery shared by Ms. Bruton; and this is reflected in the difference in our conclusions and recommendations. I am here to give my testimony on "Eritrea: A Neglected Regional Threat" and I will try to explain how the unconditional engagement of Eritrea recommended by some will actually make the region even more dangerous.

The Outcome of Unconditional Engagement

To start with, the reason the Eritrean regime is as bad as it is—topping the list of every human rights organization (GO and NGO alike) for its abysmal record—is precisely because for 8 long years, the United States and Western Europe gave it unconditional support. This is between 1991 and 1998 when the new government was given the benefit of doubt. The Clinton Administration provided military assistance, facilitated low-interest loans and grants, and contributed in capacity building and praised the autocratic system routinely, calling it part of the African Renaissance, a short-lived description praising the heads of states of Ethiopia, Uganda, Rwanda, Congo and Eritrea.   And what was the outcome? Ethiopia is what you see in the headlines now. The leaders of Uganda and Rwanda amended their constitution to extend their rule. Congo descended into civil war. And it is during that period of unconditional engagement that all the atrocities that the Eritrean regime is infamous for—arbitrary arrests, disappearances, banning religious organizations, exiling, severe restrictions on civil liberties—were germinated.

Since the subject at hand is the threat the regime poses to the region, I will focus on Eritrea's past and current relationships with its neighbors, international community, and specifically with the US. I will also show the nexus between this and how Eritrea treats its citizens—which is the subject of the UN's Special Rapporteur on Human Rights as well as another UN body instituted by its Human Rights Council, the Commission of Inquiry on Human Rights in Eritrea (CoIE).

I also will address at some length the little-known role of Nevsun, the Canadian mining company, as it has finally disclosed that it has been funding the Atlantic Council's campaign for the last 18 months to rehabilitate Eritrea's image and is calling for unconditional US engagement in Eritrea – a policy that has been tried and failed.

Eritrea's Military Adventures

Since its independence in 1991, the Eritrean regime has adopted a militarized approach to resolving disputes with its neighbors. It has waged war with Yemen, Sudan, Djibouti, Ethiopia, and inserted itself in the Somalian civil war by establishing links with Al-Shabab, which pledged allegiance to Al-Qaeda and is designated as a terrorist organization by the international community.

The latter is worth special attention if only because it is the most recent and because it sheds light on how the Eritrean regime responds better to the stick rather than the carrot. As recently as last year, some of its defenders—including Ms. Bronwyn Bruton of the Atlantic Council—were categorically denying that the regime provided ANY support to Al-Shabab.[1] Now, they are reluctantly conceding that it did—while minimizing the spoiler role it had in Somalia. More importantly, to this date, the Eritrean regime denies it ever had a role and would rather focus the world's attention not on several years' worth of reports of the United Nation's Monitoring Group on Somalia and Eritrea (SEMG) which concluded that there was substantial evidence that it did, but on new reports that there is no evidence that it still is providing support. What gets left unsaid is this: *Eritrea's overt involvement in Somalia has diminished only because it has come under scrutiny by the monitoring group and sanctioned by the International Community. Eritrea's admission last year that it has Djibouti prisoners of war and is returning them followed years of denial that it has POWs and even now, it is saying "we gave you the living", leaving the door open that it has dead POWs it hasn't accounted for.*

The supporters of the Eritrean regime are also quick to use Ethiopia and the United States as convenient deflections to justify the catastrophic mistakes of the regime. This is belied by the facts and here are some examples:

Firstly, as an Eritrean American, I have talked to hundreds of Eritreans who have joined the large exodus of the young out of the country. Not one person blames Ethiopia or the United States for their decision to leave the country. They blame the regime's indefinite military service and its gross human rights abuses.

Secondly, let's consider: after a decade of failed attempts to convince Eritrea to cooperate with the international community, especially on the war against terror, the UN Security Council, citing Eritrea's refusal to resolve a border dispute with Djibouti and its spoiler role in Somalia, imposed sanctions and arms embargo on Eritrea. Now consider this: It was the

Inter-Government Agency for Development (IGAD)—a regional organization grouping Kenya, Uganda, Somalia, Sudan, Djibouti, Eritrea and Ethiopia--and the African Union (AU), the continental congress which historically opposed sanctions against a member state, who initiated the UN sanction. It was the AU, not Ethiopia single-handedly, which deemed Eritrea's spoiler role in support of Al-Shabab and against the African Union Mission in Somalia (ANISOM), as a threat to regional peace and security and unanimously called on the Security Council to impose sanctions against Eritrea. This was remarkable because the last time the AU (formerly known as OAU) made similar request against its member state was in 1974 against the apartheid regime in South Africa. Subsequently, the US unilaterally imposed travel ban and asset freeze of Eritrean government officials, including Yemane Gebreab, Presidents Isaias's advisor and spokesperson. In 2009, President Obama signed an executive order putting Eritrea in the league of "human trafficking" nations and imposing a series of financial sanctions against it.

The Eritrean regime and its supporters' spin that all of this was the direct outcome of hostilities by Ethiopia and the United States is an insult to IGAD, an outrage against AMISOM, and an offense to the AU. It shows that, to this date, the regime has not taken responsibilities for its actions. A regime that never admits its catastrophic miscalculations and refuses to learn from them should not be rewarded with unconditional engagement, especially when the regime's regional destabilization role is ongoing.

The UN Monitoring Group on Somalia and Eritrea (SEMG) has provided evidence that shows Eritrea's continued involvement in destabilizing Somalia by threatening its international community-supported fragile government through financial support of a network of political agents and warlords with links to Al-Shabab. For the last three years, the Eritrean regime has been denying such links and refuses to cooperate with the SEMG, just as it refused to co-operate with the UN's Rapporteur on Human Rights, just as it refuses to co-operate with the UN's Commission of Inquiry on Human Rights. Nonetheless, even now, Eritrea has not denied what it calls its political and diplomatic support for such groups as it considers them as part and parcel of the Somalian people and thus, it has asserted even after they pledged allegiance to Al-Qaeda, they should have a role in the future of Somalia.

The regime's destabilization effort is not restricted to Somalia. Last June, Djibouti accused Eritrea of fomenting destabilizing activities in the region through its support of an armed opposition group. According to the most recent SEMG report, Eritrea hosts several Ethiopian armed opposition groups who frequently cross the heavily-militarized border with Ethiopia and wage attacks against Ethiopia, which are invariably followed by Ethiopian military responses. Ethiopia also hosts armed Eritrean opposition groups who also wage attacks inside Eritrea. With Ethiopia's refusal to abide by the international tribunal's decision to demarcate the border and the ever-increasing military escalations, the region will remain a flash point. It is only a matter of time before these skirmishes flare up into a full-scale war.

There is also another neglected threat that requires immediate attention:

According to the 2013 SEMG report, before switching sides in the Yemen conflict, Eritrea was training Houthi rebel groups with the help of Iran. Given the toxic relationship between Eritrea and Ethiopia, the Eritrean regime's joining of the Saudi Arabian alliance— grouping all of the Gulf States in the war against Houthi rebels—is likely to result in counter-moves by Ethiopia which has historically viewed the presence of Gulf Arab on its doorstep as an existential threat. The Ethiopian Prime Minister has warned that Ethiopia may have to take disproportionate measures to eliminate this threat. This doesn't just mean inviting Israel, Turkey to the region—which Ethiopia already has done—but military strikes.

It would be one thing if Eritrea's foreign policy was the outcome of the consensus opinion of Eritreans, it is not. Similar to its domestic policy, Eritrea's foreign policy is concentrated under one man: President Isaias Afwerki. This is the same president that the former US Ambassador to Eritrea, Ronald McMullen, described as an unhinged dictator and Eritrea as being one bullet away from implosion. In January 2013, in an incident dubbed as "Forto 2013", a group of high-ranking officers, inspired by the Arab Spring, seized the Eritrean TV station for eight hours and called for democratic reforms and the release of political prisoners. They were persuaded by other senior officers to return to their barracks with a promise of addressing their concerns, but as they were retreating they were killed in a shootout with President Isaias' security forces.

Eritrea 2016

The true picture of Eritrea does not come from people who visit Asmara, nor—with all due respect—from the diplomatic community that is quarantined in the capital and not permitted to travel more than 25 kilometers. It doesn't come from people who are given guided tours by government officials. Just as the US should not form opinions about the Horn of Africa based on input from one country, "Eritrea experts" shouldn't form opinions about the country by speaking to government officials. The truest picture of Eritrea comes from the ordinary Eritreans.

Now here, it is easy to dismiss the testimony of people like me who haven't been to Eritrea recently. It is standard practice in academic circles to put a premium on research, which is field-based. But what if people "in the field" are terrified to speak their minds? What if the field comes to you and you don't have to go to the field? This is exactly what is happening in Eritrea:

According to the authoritative United Nations High Commission for Refugees (UNHCR), by mid-2015, there were 363,167 Eritrean refugees and asylum-seekers all over the world[2]. UNHCR says that this was an increase of over 17,000 over a six-month period.

Given the Eritrean census which is estimated to be around 3 million, this is astounding. On a per-capita basis, it is one of the highest, if not the highest in the world. Now, what accounts for this?

To hear the explanations given by the Eritrean regime or its apologists, it is because of Ethiopia and the lack of border demarcation, the magnetic power of Europe, or as one explained, it is no different than Puerto Ricans moving to the United States. [3] It's surreal to hear people trot out Human Rights Watch and Amnesty International when they want to highlight Ethiopia's human rights record, yet to dismiss these same sources when they accurately describe Eritrea's human rights record as even worse.

Two-thirds of the Eritrean refugees and asylum-seekers are housed in neighboring Ethiopia and Sudan, with a substantial number in Israel. Remember, these numbers, as extraordinarily high as they are, account only for those that are registered with UNHCR. In the case of Eritreans in Sudan, the numbers are estimated to be much higher, many of whom have never been registered, and of those who registered, tens of thousands have been in refugee camps, unable to return to their homes, for generations: that is long, long before the "border dispute" with Ethiopia.

And what are the stories they tell? Well, we don't have to guess: they told their horrifying stories in hundreds of pages compiled by the UN's Commission of Inquiry on Human Rights in Eritrea (CoIE.) The atrocities were so horrific the Commission concluded that they amount to crimes against humanity. They concluded: "Eritrean officials have committed the acts of enslavement, imprisonment, enforced disappearance, torture, reprisals...inhumane acts, persecution, rape and murder."

A Unitary State In A Multi-Ethnic, Multi-Faith Society

The façade of the unitary state made up of "one people, one heart" is just that; it is no different from what every tyrant has tried to show: that, elections or not, the people stand as one in support of their government and, in my absence, the country will implode. But absent any studies—no data but anecdotal chit-chat with government officials (who have a vested interest in saying so) and multinational mining companies like Nevsun (who have a vested interest in saying so)--what we know is that underneath the surface, the country has never been as polarized as it is right now: by religion and ethnicity. For a Westerner who doesn't know the local language of Eritrea to make an assessment of "one people, one heart" or that all the people, regardless of their diversity, support the government is akin to a non-Muslim visiting Iraq during the Saddam era and reporting that the Sunnis and Shias are in perfect harmony.

To put it bluntly, the Government of Isaias Afwerki is no different than any other tyrant who finds security by creating a clique of people who are identical to him: by heritage, language, ethnicity and religion. And, like all tyrants before him, President Isaias Afwerki has been able to hide the nature of the extremely narrow support and power base he relies on by making all discussions of the subject a taboo. The power base was degraded to its present (and dangerous) stage following a series of purges that President Isaias has engineered over the last 25 years and the Eritrean regime derives its rule now by fear and terror, a policy that has exacerbated religious and ethnic tensions.

Like the rest of Africa, Eritrea is a multi-ethnic and multi-faith country which is a product of a colonizing power. Africans, after the costly experiments of unitary states which resulted in civil wars, have settled on a formula: a federal system. In fact, almost 2/3 of Africa has a Federal type of arrangement for power-sharing and equitable distribution. The Eritrean unitary state is where Africa was in the 1960s and at its current projectile, it is likely to face the same disastrous fate as it continues to deny the marginalization of ethnic groups, some to near extinction.

Nevsun's PR Campaign

In this part of my testimony, I will try to show how the interests of mining companies operating in Eritrea, specifically Nevsun, have become intertwined with that of the Issias regime.

Nevsun Resources, a Canadian mining company, and the Eritrean Government (through its mining concern ENAMCO) jointly own the Bisha Mining Share Company (BMSC). The sub-contractors of the Bisha project—Bisha is a region in Western Eritrea whose population has been permanently displaced and lives in Sudanese refugee camps for generations--are Eritrean government-owned entities that depend on the forced labor of Eritrean conscripted youth who are forcefully deployed to work with the government-owned companies. The two main subcontractors are Seghen (construction) and Horn (transportation).

Since gold production started at Bisha in 2010, Nevsun, whose stock is traded at the New York and Toronto Exchanges, has failed to:

- Have its stock value appreciate above an average of $3.50 a share in the last four years, which is considerably low for a firm that is sitting in a $1.3 billion asset, but is expected due to the political and country risk of Eritrea,
- Be acquired by a larger mining firm,
- Diversify its single source revenue from Bisha,
- Impress investors and shareholders by glossy unaudited corporate responsibility and environmental reports,
- Shake off its reputation as an enabler of human rights abusing regime ,
- Convince human right organization that it no longer uses salve labor,
- Comply with UNSEG's request to disclose financial transaction records,
- Bring any meaningful economic betterment to the lives of Eritreans other than enriching the coffers the regime.

So, Nevsun sought to rehabilitate Eritrea's image instead, knowing that its efforts were hampered by Eritrea's dismal human record. Nevsun quickly settled multiple lawsuits paying out close to $30 million, hired a public relations firm and a human rights attorney, courted the diplomatic community in Asmara – but all its efforts had failed.

When all its overt attempts failed to make a dent, Nevsun turned to a more subtle approach of funding the Atlantic Council to rehabilitate its image and that of Eritrea and lobby on its behalf.

Militarized Commerce

Since it ended the gold production phase and moved to copper production, which requires more logistical support and infrastructure to export, Nevsun has relied on the Eritrean Ministry of Defense to provide it with slave labor for mining and security, and transportation services to move its production to the port of Massawa.

Every year, the Eritrean government rounds up about 20,000 eleventh grade students (16 to 18 year olds) to finish senior high school in Sawa military camp after which most—excepting a tiny minority who get the grades to transfer to colleges--are conscripted. The overwhelming majority of the youth are sent to work for the ruling party's companies which supply slave labor to Nevsun and other companies.

For the past four years, in anticipation of the need to transport copper across Eritrea, the Eritrean military has been using forced labor to make substantial road improvement and maintenance necessary to handle the massive truck traffic moving over Eritrea's often narrow and winding escarpment roads.

The slave labor is extracted from conscripted Eritrean youth in programs overseen by the Ministry of Defense. The appointment of Sebhat Ephrem, Eritrea's former Defense Minister who is now the Minister of Energy & Mining, underscores Eritrea's crucial reliance on mining revenues. (The former minister of energy and mining, Ahmed Haj Ali, was arrested following the Forto incident of January 2013 allegedly for having a role in it. Like everyone who is made to disappear, he has not been brought to a court of law.)

With payment of close to half a billion dollars in the last four years to Eritrea, Nevsun has become a financial savior to the ruling party whose grip to power relies primarily on mining revenues from Nevsun.

Nevsun has always denied the presence of military units in Bisha mines. However, according to WikiLeaks cable from Asmara, *"Eritrea's government gave Nevsun a security team of 2000 persons, permanently stationed in the Bisha area"*.

According to an international law expert, this mutually agreed upon engagement effectively renders Nevsun activities as engaging in militarized commerce and risks assuming the liability of these abuses by stating that, *"Nevsun's officers would not be immune to criminal prosecution or civil litigation in Canada or elsewhere for abuses committed by security forces overseas."*

Modern Day Slavery

A lawsuit filed against Nevsun alleges that Nevsun used salve labor to build the Bisha mine. The lawsuit, which was filed in Canada, where Nevsun has its corporate office, was apparently encouraged by the extensive report issued by Human Rights Watch on January 3, 2013. The report under the title [4], "Hear no Evil: Forced Labor and Corporate Responsibility in Eritrea's Mining Sector," stated that, *"Nevsun's experiences show that by developing projects in Eritrea, mining firms are walking into a potential minefield of human rights problems. Most notably they risk getting entangled in the Eritrean government's uniquely abusive program of indefinite forced labor—the inaptly-named national service program."*

Nevsun's CEO, Cliff Davis, has denied the allegation of using slave labor though an entire generation of Eritreans whose labor was forcefully extracted under the guise of "national service" bear testimony to the injuries. In the past, whenever a lawsuit was filed against Nevsun, Mr. Davis was quick to state that his company will "vigorously defend itself" only to settle out of court few months later.

Nevsun has been adamantly denying accusation of violating human rights of Eritreans and damaging the country's environment. However, deposition of former employees indicate that wells in the Bisha region are depleted of deep sweet water and wells now yield only salty water.

Indigenous residents of the area who have been stranded in Sudanese camps for over four decades lament at the graves of their ancestors that were unearthed to make way for Bisha's open-pit mines.

Gift to Atlantic Council

In replying to the questions of the French journalist and writer, Léonard Vincent, Nevsun admitted to offering monetary "contribution to the Atlantic Council last year because [it was] impressed by their ongoing constructive work on Eritrea."

Mr. Vincent has asked whether Nevsun Resources, the Canadian mining company, has sponsored Ms. Bronwyn Bruton's Atlantic Council. Nevsun stated the following:

> "Nevsun made a contribution to the Atlantic Council last year because we were impressed by their ongoing constructive work on Eritrea. It is standard for a [for] profit company to make a gift to a research institute whose work relates to its business. "

In early 2015, Ms. Burton suddenly appeared as a fierce defender of the Eritrean regime whose image she has been attempting to polish while the world community is still debating at the UN whether to refer the same regime to the International Criminal Court (ICC). Until today, Ms. Burton has never disclosed that her work is funded by Nevsun.

Meanwhile, way before the Commission of Inquiry on Human Rights in Eritrea (CoIE) completed its investigation, Ms. Burton has been extensively writing to cast doubts on the CoIE findings and attempting to promote the now too-exposed regime of Eritrea that rules with impunity, unelected, since the independence of Eritrea in 1991.

In her New York Times article, Ms. Burton appears to suggest that the report of CoIE has wildly exaggerated the abuses of the government (" it's bad but not that bad" as the title had it) while at the same time saying that the CoIE barely scratched the surface and it is actually worse. Well, what is it? And what exactly is her basis for saying so: has she, for example, visited any of the Eritrean prisons or spoken to exiled Eritreans?

Yet, at private events and rallies organized by the regime's operative in the US to drum up support for Issias, Ms. Bruton makes no secret of her admiration of Issias while denouncing US policy in the Horn of Africa. Her photo and that of the VP of Nevsun, who often accompanies her to these rallies, is seen in the Facebook pages of regime supports as she has become the darling of Issias admirers.

As my colleague at awate.com, Saleh Younis, wrote, for an Africa Expert, there is a formula. If the US has a bad relationship with an African country, you advise that the US reconsider its position; if the US has a good relationship with an African country, you also advise that the US reconsider its position.

> For example, the US has a bad relationship with Somalia. So Ms. Bruton wrote an essay entitled: "Somalia: A New Approach." The keywords used in new approaches are "reboot", "reset", "rethink", "reconsider." For example, the US relationship with Kenya was deteriorating after Kenya's election. J. Peter Pham just described Kerry's visit to Kenya as "reset of the relationship." In contrast, the US has a good relationship with Ethiopia. Following the formula, Ms. Bruton wrote an essay entitled: "US Policy Shift Needed In Ethiopia." (The one that made the Eritrean government officials her fans.) In "US Policy Shift Needed In Ethiopia", Ms. Bruton argued that the US should not be

supporting a government that imprisons journalists and provides no political space to its opposition and does not have an independent civil society. Sounds good to me. But in its Eritrea equivalent (let's call it: US Policy Shift Needed in Eritrea), she is recommending that the US engage Eritrea DESPITE the fact that its treatment of journalists and opposition is much worse than that of Ethiopia. There is no civil society period in Eritrea and elections, as she said knowingly after she was so charmed by the intelligence of Isaias Afwerki, "won't happen any time soon."

When you consider the fact that there are now over a dozen mining companies in various stages of approval to prospect in Eritrea, and when you also consider the fact that many of these mining companies are Chinese which are not responsive to human rights concerns, it is clear that, engagement or no engagement with the regime, the enslavement of Eritrean youth will continue without interruption. The formula is simple and easy to predict: More mining companies, more youth enslaved, more exodus, more refugees, more asylum seekers emptying out the country. This being the case, why would the United States want to sully its considerable reputation by aligning with a government that relies on slave labor?

Concluding remarks and Recommendations

Eritrea is a mineral-rich country strategically located in the Horn of Africa and the Red Sea, where the US has vital strategic interests and legitimate concerns in its ongoing counterterrorism campaign. Hence, the US strategic interest should not depend on the fate of one ailing man, particularly when dealing with a regime that not only doesn't share any of the values that the US enshrines but routinely mocks them. While recognizing that the Eritrean people's challenges could only be solved by Eritreans, it is prudent for the US to be prepared to deal not with how to rehabilitate President Isaias Afwerki, who has no support in Eritrea and rules by fear, but with a post-Isaias Eritrea by taking the following steps aimed at shortening the sufferings of the Eritrean people and safeguarding US interests in the region:

1) To deny President Isaias the excuse to maintain a war footing, pressure Ethiopia to allow the demarcation of the border and to proceed at least in the 95% of the undisputed border areas,
2) To continue making human rights issues a precondition for US –Eritrea relations,
3) To continue supporting the current UN-sponsored sanctions against Eritrea, until the conditions for its lifting are met,
4) To support the UN Security Council members' initiatives in order to refer the UN Human Rights' Commission of Inquiry report to the International Criminal Court,
5) To provide humanitarian assistance to Eritrean refugees and to provide immigrant visas to help them come to the US and ask other countries to do the same,
6) To provide Temporary Protective Status for Eritrean refugees who are already in the US,
7) To support regional organizations' and governments' efforts in combatting human trafficking in the Horn of Africa.
8) To sanction mining companies like Nevsun that are engaged in militarized commerce and are using conscript labor force, by designating their production as conflict minerals.

> People who suffer under totalitarian regimes look up to the world community, especially the United States, for support; they become disappointed—disillusioned, when they discover misinformed consultants in a position to advise governments.

Europe has taken the position that it deals with human rights violators all over Africa and it shouldn't make that its litmus test on its engagement policy. But as its borders continue to be flooded by Eritreans escaping the police state of Eritrea, it will come to regret its decision. In any event, even the most extreme human rights violators in Africa do not enslave their youth, the way the Eritrean regime does.

It is disheartening to see aggressive approaches to absolve a totalitarian regime by individuals who have no personal stake in the outcome and only are interested to promote their careers and personal advancement.

The liberal democratic force in Eritrea has a great potential to grow, but attempts to bury it in its infancy by using the 'there-is-no-viable-opposition' claim is a crime against the Eritrean people. I urge this august body not to repeat the mistake committed during the Clinton era, when the Eritrean dictator was hailed as a renaissance leader and provided with all sorts of support, a lifeline that has helped it grow to the monster that he has become.

I urge this august body to take the right decision, decision inspired by American values. I urge you to remain a beacon of hope for the young democratic force, inspire them with the right decision, with the much-wronged Eritrean citizen in mind.

Thank You

_____

1. Bruton interview with Voice of America, Press Conference USA, http://www.voanews.com/audio/2734041.html

2. http://popstats.unhcr.org/en/demographics

3. http://www.atlanticcouncil.org/blogs/new-atlanticist/what-the-un-gets-wrong-about-rights-in-eritrea

4. https://www.hrw.org/report/2013/01/15/hear-no-evil/forced-labor-and-corporate-responsibility-eritreas-mining-sector

5. http://www.nytimes.com/2016/06/24/opinion/its-bad-in-eritrea-but-not-that-bad.html?_r=0

Mr. SMITH. Thank you so very much, Dr. Beshir.

I would like to now go to Ms. Bruton for her testimony.

STATEMENT OF MS. BRONWYN BRUTON, DEPUTY DIRECTOR, AFRICA CENTER, ATLANTIC COUNCIL

Ms. BRUTON. Thank you. I am grateful to Congressman Smith, the chair and Congresswoman Bass, the ranking member, for allowing me to contribute to the subcommittee's timely review of U.S. policy toward Eritrea.

I have had the opportunity to travel to Eritrea several times in the last 18 months. I have met repeatedly with senior officials in the country and I have had an opportunity to meet once with President Isaias for a long meeting in which we spoke very candidly about the state of affairs in Eritrea and about the state of U.S. relations with Eritrea.

What I am presenting is a summary of my written testimony and I ask that my written testimony be entered into the record.

Mr. SMITH. Without objection, yours and all of our witnesses today. Without objection.

Ms. BRUTON. Thank you. I imagine we'll talk about Nevsun later on so I would like to use my brief spoken remarks to raise a flag of caution.

I, as you mentioned, am a Somalia expert and I want to briefly turn our attention back to Somalia in 2006. When the United States accepted Ethiopia's allegations that the Union of Islamic Courts was an evil regime—an entity that was controlled by al-Qaeda—and as a result of that we allowed or perhaps more than allowed Ethiopia to invade Somalia, in doing so they destroyed the only legitimate grassroots governance movement that has ever emerged in that country, at least since independence on the 1960s.

Not only that, we cleared a space for al-Shabaab and we created the conditions in which it prospered and is now a terrorist organization that is spreading carnage across east Africa.

I raise this because I feel it is important for us to remember that though we do our best, we in the United States are capable of catastrophic mistakes when it comes to the Horn of Africa, and I want to particularly point out that all of the conditions that led us to make those mistakes in Somalia in 2006 pertain to our discussion of Eritrea today.

When it comes to Eritrea, unfortunately we are also guilty of a bias to the Ethiopian point of view. I saw that bias evident in my respected colleague, the Assistant Secretary's, remarks when she was asked about the reason for the Ethiopia-Eritrea conflict and she failed to note that Ethiopia is in violation of international law.

There is a firm and final binding of an international border commission set up in the Hague that says very clearly that Ethiopia is illegally occupying Eritrean territory.

We need to accept that, and our refusal to do so is, I think, a fairly clear sign of our bias toward the Ethiopian point of view.

That led to an error in Somalia that cost us dearly. As in 2006, I wish to remind us that it had been about 10 years since we'd had eyes on the ground in Somalia and our intelligence was very poor.

In Eritrea today, it has also been about a decade since we have had eyes on the ground in that country and our intelligence is very poor.

When I planned to go to Eritrea 18 months ago I met with a large number of government officials and members of our intelligence community and when I asked a particularly brilliant member of our intelligence committee who had studied Eritrea for 10 years, what I should be alert for when I went to the country she told me this: Find out if there is a government in Eritrea outside of Asmara.

Now, we've heard from our human rights community, who rightly expresses concern about the terrible state of affairs in that country, that the government exercises pervasive control over every aspect of life.

But we also have people in our intelligence community, and I would agree with their assessment, who wonder if the government really has any control at all outside of the capital city.

That is a worrying state of affairs and I think that it should cause us to exercise a real caution. I've heard a large number of statements today that were presented uncomplicatedly as fact but which I am aware of are hot topics of dispute within the intelligence and analytic community that if had the time I would go over them. But I've certainly highlighted most of them in my written testimony.

Finally, I want to express that I was in Somalia in 2006 and I feel we have a bit of tunnel vision in Eritrea. It's an immensely complicated country with real security concerns and a real problem with its much more powerful neighbor.

But the vast majority of our conversation is about human rights.

It's okay and it is well and good that we should discuss human rights. But those concerns should be addressed proportionately.

All the countries in the Horn of Africa have hideous human rights problems including our closest ally, Ethiopia, and I think that when we single out Eritrea for concern we raise the real possibility that our views will be either regarded as hypocritical or else, in other cases, muted because of our counterterror concerns and that does damage to our standing in the Horn of Africa.

In Eritrea, we can't afford to get it wrong, as we did in Somalia, because Eritrea is more strategically positioned on the Horn of Africa than Somalia is. It's right across from Yemen.

It's on a critically important trade route that accepts trillions of dollars a year in the passage of goods between China and the E.U.

If we get it wrong there, the impact on U.S. relations will be terrible and that will not serve our interests. Focusing on Eritrea as a threat to our interests instead of recognizing that in fact we don't recognize that it actually plays an important role as a wall through which bad actors in the Horn of Africa are not permitted to pass through to bad actors in the Gulf is important.

It's a commonality that we can use to work with Eritrea and to constructively address the concerns that we have about human rights. I think I've heard consensus from a lot of people today that engaging the government in some way would be a good idea.

I do not argue for nonconditional engagement with Eritrea, for the record. But I do believe that we could do a lot better and, for the record, I would like to state that I think a congressional delegation to Eritrea to examine the complexity of the issues that they are facing for yourselves would be a very, very good start.

I thank you for permitting me to testify.

[The prepared statement of Ms. Bruton follows:]

Bronwyn Bruton
Deputy Director, Africa Center at the Atlantic Council

**Hearing Before the House Committee on Foreign Affairs,
Subcommittee on Africa, Global Health, Global Human Rights, and International
Organizations**

2:00 p.m., Wednesday, September 14, 2016
Room 2172, Rayburn House Office Building, Washington, DC

"Eritrea: A Neglected Regional Threat"

* * *

I am grateful to Congressman Smith, the chair, and Congresswoman Bass, the ranking member, for allowing me to contribute to the Subcommittees' timely review of U.S. policy towards Eritrea. My remarks will describe the current state of affairs inside Eritrea as they relate to US interests in the Horn of Africa. And I will offer some practical suggestions on how the United States might put its relations with Eritrea on a more constructive footing. I had a long meeting with Eritrea's President Isaias Afwerki in February 2015, and we discussed Eritrea's relations with the United States at some length. Over the past 18 months I have continued to engage regularly with the Eritrean government, traveling periodically to Asmara, and communicating regularly with American and European diplomats, human rights researchers, United Nations' officials, and of course the Eritrean diaspora.

The ground is shifting rapidly in the Horn of Africa. Recent events next door to Eritrea, in Ethiopia, have laid bare the fundamental brutality and instability of the government that the United States has used, for years, as its indispensable ally in the region. In recent months, more than 500 peaceful protestors have been gunned down by Ethiopian security forces on the streets of the Oromo and Amhara regions. Since October of last year, more than 10,000 people have been arrested and/or interrogated and/or tortured.[1] Many of these victims have been young students. And less than two weeks ago, at least 23—and probably many more—political prisoners died violently inside the Kilinto prison on the outskirts of Addis Ababa.
These events pose a significant and immediate threat to regional security, as an influx of even a million Ethiopian refugees into Somaliland, South Sudan or Eritrea would overwhelm those territories.

Eritrea, on the other hand, poses no obvious threat to US interests. International depictions of Eritrea as a "regional spoiler" have seemed overblown for years – as evidenced by the reporting of the United Nations' Somalia and Eritrea Monitoring Group. (For the past three years, the

---

[1] Human Rights Watch. "Such a Brutal Crackdown: Killings and Arrests in Response to Ethiopia's Oromo Protests," June 16, 2016, https://www.hrw.org/report/2016/06/16/such-brutal-crackdown/killings-and-arrests-response-ethiopias-oromo-protests.

SEMG has found no evidence of significant violations of international law committed by Eritrea, and I understand that the SEMG's upcoming report, due in November, will be no different in this regard.)

On the contrary, a number of surprising and positive developments have recently been occurring in Eritrea, suggesting that the country is determined to throw off the isolation that has characterized most of the "no peace, no war" period. This is very good news for the region; and if the United States can encourage Eritrea along this trajectory, it should. But to do that, Washington will have to drop outdated notions about the threat that Eritrea poses. At a time when the Kenyan army has annexed parts of southern Somalia and is trafficking with al Shabaab, when the Ugandan army is taking sides in South Sudan, and the Ethiopian army is shooting and arresting thousands of innocent protestors, Eritrea truly ranks among the least of the United States' security concerns.

A disordered Ethiopia will make Eritrea more important to US security interests. By virtue of its geographic position between Ethiopia and Yemen, Eritrea is bound to serve either as a bridge or a barrier to the passage of bad actors between the Persian Gulf and the Horn of Africa. Thus far, Eritrea has proved to be a strong barrier to the spread of radical ideologies. This is a role for which it has received little credit. But Washington cannot afford to take Eritrea's implicit cooperation in its counterterror efforts for granted.

If Eritrea is overwhelmed with refugees, or otherwise sucked into Ethiopia's growing unrest, the United States could find itself facing instability and perhaps a terror threat on both sides of the critical Mandeb Strait, which is a chokepoint for the trillions of dollars of trade passing between the European Union and Asia. Threats to this trade route have in recent years led the United States to pour billions on billions of dollars into combating Somali piracy – an indication of the trade route's importance to US interests.

For these reasons, the US ought to be concerned about its inability to project influence inside Eritrea's territory. I hope that this hearing may offer the Congress and the incoming Administration some useful insight into how to improve the relationship with Asmara.

INTRODUCTION: The state of Eritrea today

Historical overview of US relations with Eritrea
In 1991, after thirty years of trench and mountain warfare, Eritrean rebels overthrew the Communist Derg regime and won its independence. The tenacity and bravery of the Eritrean rebels captured the hearts and imaginations of people across the globe, but their independence was accepted only grudgingly by the United States, which had been instrumental in denying Eritrea's independence and forcing it into federation with Ethiopia after the second World War. The period between 1991 and 1998 were watershed years for the country: a referendum establishing Eritrea's independence was held, a democratic constitution was written, and Eritrea's economy prospered.

But separation from Ethiopia proved impossible. By 1996, a collection of small, unavoidable disputes between the two countries (over such matters as the regulation of cross-border trade, the creation of an Eritrean currency, and the demarcation of the border) had piling up, adding tension to a more substantive disagreement between President Isaias and Prime Minister Meles Zenawi, over Ethiopia's decision to pursue a model of ethnic "federalism."[2] In 1998, only seven years after the end of Eritrea's thirty-year battle for independence, these many differences escalated into a full-scale war between the countries that lasted for two years and killed some 90,000 people.

The Ethiopia-Eritrea border war ended when both sides agreed to sign the Algiers Agreement, which established both a cease-fire and an independent border commission in The Hague (called the Eritrea-Ethiopia Boundary Commission, or EEBC). The United States, the European Union, the Organization of African Unity (now called the African Union) and the United Nations signed the Algiers Agreement as witnesses. As it was desperately attempting to broker a peace, the United States apparently made closed-door promises to both sides that it would serve as guarantor to the EEBC's ruling. But when the EEBC eventually awarded most of the disputed border territory to Eritrea—including the flashpoint town of Badme—Ethiopia reneged on the agreement, and the witnesses to the treaty did nothing. Since then, for the past 15 years, Ethiopian troops have been permitted by a silent international consensus to flout the treaty and illegally occupy Eritrean territory. In consequence, the border between the two countries is heavily militarized and skirmishes occasionally claim lives. And Eritrea has been trapped in a painful stasis known as "no peace, no war."

Ethiopia's refusal to comply with the firm and final ruling of the Boundary Commission is the primary source of instability in East Africa. Both Ethiopia and Eritrea have supported armed rebel groups across the region, in efforts to destabilize each other's territory through proxy warfare. Eritrea has exhibited especially poor judgement in its choice of proxies: One of the groups that it supported early on was the al Shabaab militia group in Somalia. By all indications, Eritrean support of al Shabaab was short-lived, insubstantial, had no visible impact on the course of events in Somalia, and occurred before that group was listed as a terrorist organization. Eritrea was nonetheless sanctioned by the UN Security Council—an effort that was spearheaded by the United States.

Ethiopia's invasion of Somalia in late 2006, and the Ethiopian army's subsequent occupation of Mogadishu, by contrast, has done immeasurable harm to US security interests.[3] Ethiopia's invasion of Somalia destroyed an innocuous and potentially constructive Somali grassroots governance movement called the Union of Islamic Courts. At the time, Ethiopia falsely alleged that the Union of Islamic Courts was a proxy of al Qaeda, and persuaded Washington to back its interpretation. When Ethiopia invaded Somalia and destroyed this moderate Union of Islamic Courts, it cleared the field for the rise of al Shabaab. Al Shabaab—which before the Ethiopian invasion was unpopular in Somalia—was able to rise to power on a wave of public fury against

---

[2] Federalism is a controversial system of government, both in Ethiopia and Somalia; it is effectively a system of ethnic segregation.

[3] Bronwyn Bruton, "Somalia: A New Approach," Council on Foreign Relations Special Report No. 52, March 2010, http://www.cfr.org/content/publications/attachments/Somalia_CSR52.pdf.

the atrocities that the Ethiopian army was committing in Mogadishu. It was the rage of the Somali people against Ethiopian and US meddling that permitted al Shabaab to become a national resistance movement; to seize most of southern Somalia's territory; and to provide the long-feared sanctuary to al Qaeda.[4] Worse still, outrage over the rapes and atrocities perpetrated by Ethiopian troops in Somalia sparked the transit of dozens of Somali Americans from Minnesota to Mogadishu, creating, for the first time, a problem of homegrown radicalization in the United States.

Ethiopia was not sanctioned for these actions; on the contrary, Washington has repeatedly praised the Ethiopian regime for its support of US counterterror efforts,[5] and since 2006 provided it with billions of dollars in economic, budgetary and humanitarian assistance. Via the African Union, the United States also provides extensive military support to Ethiopia in return for its deployment of troops to Somalia.

The asymmetry of the United States' treatment of these two countries has created a reasonable perception among Eritrean officials that Washington is "hostile" to Eritrea and directly responsible for many aspects of the country's suffering over the past 18 years. Eritrea is even more concerned about American hostility than it is about Ethiopia. As Eritrea's senior presidential advisor, recently commented: "The problem with Eritrea is not Ethiopia; it is the United States."[6] President Isaias expressed the same conviction when I met with him in February 2015.

Over the years, US rhetoric has helped to establish a fictional dichotomy between the "good" Ethiopia and the "spoiler" Eritrea. This dichotomy is not based on objective fact, and thus has a detrimental effect on US credibility in Africa. The US condemnation of Eritrea and its failure to respond to Ethiopian military adventurism, poor governance, and human rights abuses is widely attributed to the useful role that Ethiopia has played in supporting US counterterrorism objectives. As a result, anti-American sentiment is rising across the Horn of Africa, but most especially in Ethiopia, where the government has imprisoned thousands of journalists, politicians, bloggers, as suspected "terrorists." US political and financial support of the Ethiopian government is widely viewed as instrumental to the regime's continuing stranglehold on power. These perceptions could easily contribute to the rooting of jihadist agenda in the Horn.

Current conditions in Eritrea
The Eritrean government has also made many mistakes. I do not mean to downplay actions that the Eritrean government has taken to support armed groups in the region, to restrict the freedom

---

[4] Bronwyn Bruton and Paul Williams, Counterinsurgency in Somalia: Lessons Learned from the African Union Mission in Somalia, 2007-2013, report no. 14-5, Joint Special Operations Universitu, ix-110.

[5] Mehari Tadele Maru, "The Secret to Ethiopia's Counter Terrorism Success," Al Jazeera, July 31, 2015, http://www.aljazeera.com/indepth/opinion/2015/07/secret-ethiopia-counterterrorism-success-150728112317438.html

[6] "INTERVIEW: Mr. Yemane Gebreab with German Reporter," RAIMOQCOM, July 15, 2016, http://www.raimoq.com/interview-mr-yemane-gebreab-with-german-reporter-oliver/.

of expression and other civil liberties within its own borders, to violate human rights, and violate norms of diplomat relations (such as the arrest of US embassy employees or the opening of diplomatic pouches). But my respected colleagues on this panel have already ensured that this information is effectively and thoroughly represented on the record.

What is so far missing from the record is the Eritrean government's point of view.

The absence of this perspective is terribly dangerous to US interests in the Horn of Africa, and beyond.

When there is poor access to a country – and there has now been a decade of poor access to Eritrea, just as there was a decade of poor access to Somalia, as of 2006 – it is painfully easy to get it wrong. And there are terrible consequences to getting it wrong in the Horn of Africa.

In my testimony I have already referred to the catastrophic series of events that Washington's misanalysis of events in Somalia triggered in 2006. Washington's missteps in 2006 occurred precisely because it listened only to Ethiopia's point of view. If Washington had back then given Asmara a seat at the table, Somalia would probably look substantially different and better today. Washington might, for example, have recognized the true nature of the Islamic Courts and resisted Ethiopia's ill-conceived attack on Somalia. As important, Washington would have had the means to engage with the right actors in Somalia: not with the liberal fringe of Islamists who gathered in Djibouti and ultimately signed the Djibouti Peace Agreement, but with the middle-of-the-spectrum Islamists, like Hassan Dahir Aweys, who had standing within their clans and who chose to gather in Asmara. Had Washington chosen to engage with those "middle of the spectrum" Islamists, the peace agreements and ceasefires might have held. Asmara said that at the time; Washington didn't listen. And the result is that today, al Shabaab is spreading carnage throughout the whole of East Africa.

The United States cannot afford to get it wrong in Eritrea, not least because that country has valuable insights to offer regarding the resolution of the conflicts in Somalia and South Sudan. And it can't afford not at least to be thinking about worst-case contingencies. If Ethiopia's instability worsens, the United States may ultimately be faced with a situation of multiple state failure in the Horn: a swath of instability that stretches from Somalia, through Ethiopia, to Yemen, through the Sudan, and onwards to the Sahel. And, in this worst-case scenario, Eritrea, Djibouti and Somaliland will be the vital buffers between that instability and the billions of dollars of trade passing everyday through the Mandeb Strait.

The good news is that the United States can still get it right. But a course correction is required.

7 Common misconceptions about Eritrea
To develop a policy towards Eritrea that will promote positive political change rather than do harm, Washington needs first and foremost to understand what is happening there.
Unfortunately, in the absence of eyes on the ground in Eritrea, a number of questionable assumptions have taken root in the policy and media debate about the country. They are:

1) The Eritrean government as fragile and unpopular, and could collapse at any time.

My research has convinced me that there is no serious opposition inside Eritrea to President Isaias or his government. There is certainly unhappiness and unspoken dissent inside Eritrea. Increasingly, that dissent is voiced aloud. But Eritreans are very much aware that there is no viable alternative to the present government, and that lack of alternatives has produced a tangible sense of resignation. Of course, as in Ethiopia, the lack of political alternatives is caused by the government's imprisonment and exile of the best and brightest of the political opposition. But it remains a fact that the Eritrean opposition is not perceived as more credible than the government, and in the case of any government collapse, a protracted and potentially violent power struggle would likely occur. Eritreans fear that possibility.

International analysts have often perceived signs that a popular uprising is imminent—many such predictions were made, for example, in the wake of the "Forto incident"[7] of 2013. But such predictions have proved inaccurate time and again; and the reality is that incidents like the one at Forto, and in Asmara in June of this year,[8] have proven extremely rare. Policymakers should note that the revolts now spreading through Ethiopia and Zimbabwe have been facilitated by reliable internet connections and a decent amount of cellphone penetration—conditions that do not currently exist in Eritrea.

Finally, Eritreans are passionately nationalistic. Despite the virulent tribal and ethnic conflicts plaguing the rest of the region, the Eritrean government appears to have been exceptionally successful in its own nation-building project. Eritreans seem largely unified across tribal and religious categories. Eritreans across the world, whether or not they support the government, demonstrate a strong sense of national identity and display pride in their country.

Given this dynamic, the United States should consider the possibility that international criticism of Eritrea—reflected in the shrill condemnations of the Isaias regime, the imposition and continuation of sanctions, the failure to enforce the Algiers Agreement, and continued silence regarding the presence of Ethiopian troops on Eritrean soil—may have very counterproductive effects on the ground. Many Eritreans take the insults directed at their government personally, and many are prone to blame Washington rather than Asmara for the current state of affairs in their country. Sanctions and other punitive devices may actually lend credence to government narratives that Eritrea is being persecuted by the international community. Such perceptions can easily lead to increased support for the government, both inside Eritrea and in the diaspora. In particular, Washington should beware that many average Eritreans recoil from human rights narratives that depict them as helpless children waiting desperately for a Western intervention.[9]

---

[7] Jeffrey Gettleman, "Coup Attempt by Rebel Soldiers is Said to Fail in Eritrea." New York Times, January 21, 2013, http://www.nytimes.com/2013/01/22/world/africa/coup-attempt-fails-in-eritrea.html?_r=0

[8] "Shots Fired, Stoning in Eritrea's Capital," Awate.com, April 5, 2016, http://awate.com/shots-fired-stoning-in-eritreas-capital/.

[9] Makau W. Mutua, "Savages, Victims, and Saviors: The Metaphor of Human Rights." Harvard International Law Journal 42, no. 1 (2001): 201-45, http://papers.ssrn.com/sol3/papers.cfm?abstract_id=1525547.

These are the same Eritreans who pride themselves on having fought down the Derg and the Ethiopian army, after all.

In short, Washington's singling out of Eritrea for criticism serves neither its diplomatic nor its governance and human rights objectives.

2) Isolation tactics can be used to pressure the Eritrean government into instituting reforms.

Mr. Isaias and his colleagues fought the Derg for thirty years and are far more comfortable now than they were then. They will be pressured into change by Western disapproval.

Further, in this multipolar global environment, it is not possible for the United States to isolate Eritrea. Sanctions, verbal condemnations of the government, the United Nation's Commission of Inquiry on Eritrea, and other such devices have simply compelled the government to give up on America, and to pivot towards China and the Gulf for support. Indeed, the success of that pivot is the primary political development of the past 18 months in Eritrea. Asmara has formed strong strategic alliances with the United Arab Emirates, Qatar and Saudi Arabia, providing a base for their counterterror efforts in the Red Sea basin. It has also scaled up its relations with Egypt, deepened ties to South Africa, and secured a series of new Chinese mining investments. These alliances are more than enough to sustain Eritrea – it is not a large country. And with blank checks starting to flow in from China and Gulf, and with strong support from the Arab world to address its own very pressing counterterror objectives, Asmara has less reason than ever to be concerned about the opinion of Washington.

3) The threat from Ethiopia is not real; the government simply uses it as an excuse to crack down on dissent.

The failure of the international community to appreciate the extent to which Ethiopia's actions have destabilized Eritrea is a serious flaw in our analysis of the Horn. The military threat from Ethiopia is real and pressing. Indeed, Ethiopian aggression towards Eritrea has been steadily escalating over the past 18 months and the increased threat of an Ethiopian annexation of Eritrean territory is a major threat to regional stability.

In March 2015, Ethiopia bombed Eritrea twice, striking a military depot in Asmara and killing eight people, and striking the perimeter fence of the Bisha mine (causing no casualties and little damage). For the record, these strikes have been confirmed on a not-for-attribution basis by officials of the Eritrean government, the US government, and the operators of the Bisha mine. Ethiopia's bombing of the Bisha site, a civilian target and a foreign-owned investment, is a clear violation of the rules of war. But neither Washington nor the UN Security Council so much as commented on the attack. Meanwhile, Ethiopia's prime minister, Hailemariam Desalegn, has repeatedly announced—both on the floor of the parliament and in Ethiopia's government-controlled press—that Ethiopia intends to attack Eritrea. [10] In June 2016, Ethiopia did exactly as it had announced, initiating a major conflict on the Eritrean border (at the area known as the

---

[10] "Ethiopian Threatens Action against Eritrea," *Sudan Tribune,* July 8, 2016. http://www.sudantribune.com/spip.php?article55622.

"Tsorona front")[11] that killed hundreds of soldiers and displaced an unknown number of civilians. Despite Ethiopia's admission that it initiated the assault, Washington has merely called for "both parties" to exercise restraint.[12]

The threat of a renewed war between Eritrea and Ethiopia is my number one concern for stability in the Horn of Africa. Washington's illogical posture towards Eritrea, and its willingness to overlook the military aggressions of its counterterror partners—such as Ethiopia's invasion of Somalia in 2006; Kenya's invasion of Somalia in 2011; Kenya's well-documented and deliberate trafficking of illegal goods with the al Qaeda-linked al Shabaab terror group in Somalia; Uganda's current incursions into South Sudan; and Ethiopia's repeated military attacks on Eritrea over the past 18 months—has created a dangerous climate of impunity that has made the renewal of the Ethiopia-Eritrea war substantially more likely.

    4) The Eritrean government can and should implement reforms before any meaningful Western development assistance or investment is provided to the regime.

For the past 18 years, Eritreans have lived with the threat of a hostile army within its borders. The presence of Ethiopian troops on Eritrean soil has done crippling harm to the Eritrean people. It has produced a state of paralysis that is generally described as "no peace, no war" – a condition of constant insecurity, a limbo in which economic and political development have proved all but impossible. The continued closure of the Ethiopia-Eritrea border has done serious damage to Eritrea's economy: prior to the border war, the vast majority of Eritrea's trade was with Ethiopia. That portion of the gross domestic product has entirely disappeared. And the effort to maintain Eritrea's defenses has continuously consumed an inordinate amount of Eritrea's budget, which in turn diminishes Eritrea's ability to develop its schools, hospitals and industries.

The presence of this "army at the gates" has of course also undermined Eritrea's political development. The over-militarization of the country as a justified means of defending the country has had severe consequences for political and civil space.

The active threat from Ethiopia has also forced the Eritrean government to extend its program of mandatory military conscription far beyond its intended duration of 18 months.

The practice of mandatory, indefinite military conscription in Eritrea (known as the "National Service") is the primary concern of human rights activists. But reforming the military conscription program will be difficult, despite the Eritrean government's public statements that it is willing to do so. Currently, nearly all public sector, and probably a majority of private sector, jobs are performed by national service conscripts working for nominal or "volunteer" wages. Asmara claims that it has raised many of these wages already (and anecdotal reports from

---

[11] Bronwyn Bruton. "A Frightening Flare-up on the Ethiopia/Eritrea Border, and Another Resounding Silence from Washington," *AfricaSource*, June 14, 2016, http://www.atlanticcouncil.org/blogs/africasource/a-frightening-flare-up-on-the-ethiopia-eritrea-border-and-another-resounding-silence-from-washington.

[12] US Department of State, "The United States Calls for Restraint on the Ethiopia-Eritrea Border," June 14, 2016, http://www.state.gov/r/pa/prs/ps/2016/06/258489.htm.

Western journalists and diplomats seem to confirm this). But fully normalizing the National Service will require the conversion of most National Service positions into civil service and private sector jobs that provide a market-based wage. Without a significant influx of development funding or investment, it is hard to see how that would be possible to achieve. This strongly suggests that development assistance to Eritrea will need to precede any meaningful reform of the National Service program – not the other way around.

5) The Eritrean government exerts pervasive and stifling control over every aspect of life in Eritrea.

In preparation for my first visit to Eritrea, I met with a range of US intelligence officers. One of these individuals was particularly well informed, having studied Eritrea for more than a decade. When I asked her what I should be alert for during my visit, and whether there was any information that she would consider helpful for her own research, she responded:

"Find out if there is a government in Eritrea, outside of Asmara."

This officer is to be commended for her thoughtful open-mindedness; but the question itself is a rather frightening indication of how very little even our intelligence community understands about the nature of government control in Eritrea.

The idea that there is no government outside of Asmara is clearly false; but equally false is the notion that Eritrea exercises a North Korea-like control over its citizens.

Through my conversations with the Western diplomats serving in Asmara, I found that they unanimously agree that the Eritrean government is among the least corrupt in Africa, and they don't doubt the government's commitment to achieving economic development for Eritrea. They do agree, however, that the government's capacity is alarmingly low. The arrest or defection of many senior members of the party over the years has left President Isaias dependent on a very small handful of trusted advisors to run the country. When one of them leaves the country, important affairs are put on hold. Migration has created a terrible problem of "brain drain" in Eritrea – so that there is a near-desperate lack of capacity in the middle and lower ranks of the bureaucracy. Eritrea has also been systematically starved of development funds and investment since the border war; so, despite its abundant natural resources, its lack of corruption, and its strategic location on the Red Sea, it is now one of the very poorest nations on earth.[13]

Given that the Eritrean government is extremely poor, deeply lacking in capacity at many levels, and profoundly dependent on involuntary military conscripts, its capacity to truly coerce the Eritrean population is probably quite limited. Assuredly, intimidation does occur, and is considered oppressive by Eritreans with whom I have spoken, both inside and outside the country. It has become clear to me, however, that government intimidation is only one of many

---

[13] As of 2015, Eritrea was ranked 186 out of 187 countries on the United Nations Development Programme's Human Development Index. See "Human Development Reports: Eritrea." United Nations Development Programme. http://hdr.undp.org/en/countries/profiles/ERI.

factors that has produced a state of "stasis"[14] or quietude in the population. Other important factors include: the state of "no peace, no war," leading many to feel that political reforms must be deferred until the nation is secured; loyalty to the liberation party, coupled with anger at the United States, and a perception that sanctions and other Western actions are responsible for Eritrea's problems; the ability of dissatisfied Eritreans to migrate from the country; the fear that the likely alternatives to President Isaias are even worse.

All of these factors contribute to the population's continued acceptance of the regime. The narrative of crushing government repression is not only too simplistic, but likely to lead Washington into policy errors.

6) The state of human rights is worse in Eritrea than it is in any other country in the region.

Though extensive human rights violations occur in Eritrea, the country is extremely stable and appears to have very low rates of crime or chronic hunger. The populations of Somalia, Sudan and South Sudan experience far higher levels of violence. In terms of repression, Eritrea is on a par with Ethiopia and Djibouti. A recent UN Human Rights Council Commission of Inquiry on Eritrea entirely failed to make the case that Eritrean human rights abuses were either systemic or the result of deliberate government policy.[15] Though Eritrea's human rights record is assuredly a concern, Eritrea is not uniquely bad when compared to the other countries of the Horn.

7) Change in Eritrea is impossible as long as President Isaias remains in power.

Despite the profound challenges that Eritrea faces, the government is attempting to emerge from the economic and political stasis of the post-border war period. In the past two years, Asmara has made serious efforts to improve its relations with European countries. It has formed new alliances with Arab and African partners, has sought to reenter the Intergovernmental Authority on Development (IGAD), and has ramped up its participation in the African Union. Approximately fifty foreign journalists have been permitted to enter and report on the country. Significantly, several foreign NGOs have been permitted to re-enter Eritrea and to open programs in the country, and one of these groups, Finn Church Aid, recently visited Sawa, a school and military training camp that has been off-limits to Westerners for about a decade and is thought be the epicenter of human rights abuses in the country. The UN Office of the High Commission for Human Rights was recently permitted to tour a prison. Eritrea has also recently released all of the living Djiboutian prisoners of war, a major development that bodes well for regional stability. The judicial code has been revised, though the changes are not yet implemented. It appears that the government is raising the salaries of National Service conscripts, which it says is the first step towards normalizing the program and converting the NS posts into civil service and private sector jobs. President Isaias has also indicated that he is in the process of writing a new constitution. (The president was clear when I met him that the new

---

[14] Richard Reid, "The Politics of Silence: Interpreting Stasis in Contemporary Eritrea." *Review of African Political Economy* 36, no. 120 (2009): 209-21, doi:10.1080/03056240903065125.

[15] Bronwyn Bruton, "It's Bad in Eritrea, but Not That Bad," *The New York Times*, June 23, 2016, http://www.nytimes.com/2016/06/24/opinion/its-bad-in-eritrea-but-not-that-bad.html.

constitution would enshrine Eritrea's current system, and would not be the result of a democratic process. But this nevertheless represent progress, as any constitution is better than none.)

Given the government's limited finances and bureaucratic capacity, progress on all of these fronts has sometime been frustratingly slow. But they are nevertheless positive steps. And Eritrea is undertaking these steps of its own accord – not as a result of foreign pressure, nor in pursuit of foreign funding, which it has often refused. Because the changes are voluntary, they have a better chance of being sustainable.

US RELATIONS WITH ERITREA

The question for the United States is what, if any, constructive role it can play in Eritrea's development.

Over the past 18 months I have engaged with the government of Asmara and the US State Department in an effort to understand the impediments to a better relationship. They are many. On the US side, they include the ongoing imprisonment of four former employees of the US embassy; the restricting of US embassy personnel to perimeter of 20 kilometers around Asmara; the opening of diplomatic pouches and the recalling of Eritrea's ambassador from the embassy in Washington; the expulsion of the US Agency for International Development; human rights abuses and the general closure of democratic space; Eritrea's holding of Djiboutian prisoners of war (though Eritrea claims to have released all of its Djiboutian prisoners, and has indeed withdrawn from Djiboutian territory in compliance with an international ruling and the mediation process being led by Qatar); Eritrea's refusal to permit the UN's Somalia and Eritrea Monitoring Group unfettered access to the country; and Eritrea's continued funding of armed groups to perpetuate its proxy conflict with Ethiopia. State Department officials will probably prefer not to acknowledge it, but there is also a clear and pervasive irritation among American officials over the fact that Eritrea, despite the firm and final ruling of the EEBC in its favor, has not simply given up on Badme and moved on.[16]

As I have noted in my introduction to this testimony, Eritrea also possesses a substantial list of grievances against the United States. These include: Washington's refusal to grant Eritrean independence following the second World War, which directly necessitated the 30-year war that killed an uncounted number of Eritreans; Washington's failure to enforce the Algiers Agreement and its apparent prioritization of Ethiopia's interests over those of Eritrea; the Washington-led effort to sanction Eritrea for its actions in Somalia and around the region; Washington's continued refusal to lift those sanctions, despite the UN Somalia and Eritrea Monitoring Group's failure to find any major violations of law by Eritrea over the past four years; Washington's travel ban and sanctions on various Eritrean officials; and finally, what is perceived as a Washington-led effort to use UN human rights instruments as a mechanism for bringing Eritrea to the International Criminal Court. (This last grievance persists despite the fact that the United

---

[16] In his memoirs, former US ambassador to the United Nations John Bolton describes the efforts of Assistant Secretary of State for African Affairs Jendayi Frazer to overturn the border ruling in Ethiopia's favor. See Michela Wrong, *America's Latest African Blunder* (Slate, November 29, 2007), available at: http://www.slate.com/articles/news_and_politics/foreigners/2007/11/americas_latest_african_blunder.html

States does not appear to support the report's forwarding to the UN Security Council.) Eritrea rightly resents the United States' refusal to hold Ethiopia accountable for its continued military aggressions, including the assaults on the border and the bombings of Eritrean territory.

The United States and Eritrea cannot repair all of these breaches overnight.

Surprisingly and importantly, however, when I met with President Isaias, he asserted that the relationship between the United States and Eritrea was fundamentally sound, and that he was himself convinced that at some point in the future, the two countries would be friends.

Friendship between the United States and Eritrea would be in the interests of both countries.

It is not well-remembered, but during the 1990s, Eritrean was a key counterterrorism partner of the United States, assisting Washington in its efforts to track Osama bin Laden's activities in the Sudan. When Secretary of Defense Donald Rumsfeld visited Eritrea in the wake of 9/11, he remarked that the US could learn a lot from Eritrea about counterterrorism.[17] Today, Eritrea has a markedly socialist bent, but it still shares many fundamental values with the United States. Eritrea's system of governance is repressive of liberties that Americans consider fundamental, but certainly not more so than Ethiopia, which has enjoyed close ties with Washington.

The only structural impediment to a better relationship is the United States' continued dependence on Ethiopia as its "anchor" in the region. But it is likely that the US relationship with Eritrea could be dramatically improved even in the absence of any substantial change in the US-Ethiopia partnership. Specific actions will be required of Washington, but the upcoming change in Administration should offer a convenient opportunity for a reset.

- President Isaias was explicitly clear during our meeting in February 2015 that he considers the lifting of the UN Security Council sanctions on Eritrea to be a precondition of any serious effort to improve relations between the two countries. These sanctions should have been lifted years ago – as noted, the UN Somalia and Eritrea Monitoring Group has found no substantial violations by Eritrea of international law. Washington should consider too that there is express desire on the part of the UN Sanctions Committee to lift the Eritrea sanctions, due to an anxiety that the continuation of sanctions in the absence of any wrongdoing will diminish the credibility of sanction regimes in general, and at a time when the impartiality of international justice mechanisms (the International Criminal Court in particular) is being widely questioned in Africa.

  Lifting the sanctions will of course require cooperation from Asmara. But nothing in my engagement with Asmara has suggested that a visit from the SEMG to Eritrea is beyond the realm of possibility—provided that Washington makes its openness to the possibility of lifting the sanctions clear.

---

[17] Jim Garamone, "Eritrea Could Teach US Much to Combat Terror," US Department of Defense News Article, December 10. 2002. http://archive.defense.gov/news/newsarticle.aspx?id=42407.

- Asmara does not expect Washington to send troops to its border to enforce the Algiers Agreement. But it would be tremendously helpful for Washington to signal its continuing commitment to the "firm and final" nature of the EEBC ruling on the border. A Congressional resolution or a simple statement from the State Department could help to accomplish that.

- Finally, Washington must learn to be more even-handed in its response to military provocations and human rights abuses in the Horn. When Ethiopia attacks Eritrea, Washington must publicly take notice. And efforts to single out Eritrea for criticism on human rights grounds must stop. (That is certainly not to say that Washington should not continue to press for human rights reforms in Eritrea – US outrage simply needs to be spread more proportionately around the Horn. And Washington needs to do this regardless of whether it wishes to improve relations with Eritrea, in order to combat the common African perception that the United States dismisses human rights and democracy concerns whenever more important counterterror objectives are in play.)

Washington has its own list of action items for Eritrea. But I believe that it is up to the United States to take the first step. Asmara has already pivoted successfully towards new alliances in the Gulf and a new economic partnership with China, and it is reluctant to invest its scarce diplomatic resources in a hopeless cause. In order to improve relations, a strong signal needs to be sent to Asmara from Washington.

Eritrea has also made great progress in improving its relations with individual European nations, and with the European Union. Because of migration, the EU has a vested interest in Eritrea's development. That makes Europe an inherently better partner for Eritrea, and Washington would be wise to let London and Brussels lead the way on development assistance.

President Isaias and his advisors will not swivel back towards Washington unless they have good reason to do so. But my own dialogue with Asmara over the past 18 months leads me to believe that President Isaias would very much like to put his relations with Washington on a more constructive footing. Given the high stakes in the Horn of Africa, and very low level of effort that would be required to set the stage for a much better relationship in the future, it is surely in Washington's interest to try.

Mr. SMITH. Ms. Bruton, thank you very much for your testimony as well.

I'd like to first ask Father Ghebre-Ab, if you could—you mentioned 2,000 to 3,000 prisoners of conscience who are incarcerated because of their faith and I wonder if you can tell us is that both men and women?

Are children included? Are they tortured? Are there attempts to coerce them to reject their faith and if so to what end, perhaps? How long are the usual sentences for a believer? Is it 5 years, 10 years, life?

And when released, where do they go? Do they leave totally impoverished with families? I often argue even in ordinary criminal justice systems when one family member goes to prison the whole family, in a way, goes to prison.

It often leads to an impoverishment. But this would seem to be even more extreme. When they come out, where do they go? So if you could perhaps speak to that.

Mr. GHEBRE-AB. It is both men and women, young and old. The condition of their imprisonment is about as horrid as one can expect.

Now, so many prisons, recognized and unrecognized, dot the landscape of Eritrea. Many times no one knows where they are. They never appear in front of a court and charged with any kind of crime and therefore no one knows when they will be coming out.

Now, particularly, for instance, I have made a list of people who have been in prison for the last 12 years now and they have never, never seen the inside of the court. They have never been charged with anything and these were, as I have explained in my longer remarks, the leading intellectuals within the Eritrean Orthodox Church. They remain in prison.

And there has always been torture, and as previously stated also, an attempt at forcing them to recant their faith. Very often, statements have been made about minority Christian and other sects.

But, really, the larger churches are not immune from this either—the so-called recognized churches. The Eritrean Orthodox Church, as I have clearly pointed out in my longer version of my presentation, has literally been taken over by the government and it has become as if it is one department of the government and the government's thinking, as I see it, is that by controlling the Eritrean Orthodox Church, which is almost 50 percent of its population, it thinks that it controls half the population of Eritrea as well.

But I would also like to point out that really the lack of religious liberty in Eritrea is only one aspect of human rights violations and if there is going to be any improvement in human rights violations we cannot really cherry pick this right and that right. It has to be—it has to be approached in its totality and the only thing that will ensure that is the implementation of the Constitution that was ratified by the people in Eritrea in 1997.

Mr. SMITH. Let me ask you, if I could, Ms. Bruton, with regards to some of the points that were raised by Dr. Beshir—just in the interest of full and total disclosure, do you or anybody that you are affiliated with derive any funding directly or indirectly from the Government of Eritrea or from Nevsun or any of its affiliates?

Ms. BRUTON. We do not derive any funding whatsoever from the Government of Eritrea. Nevsun, which is a publicly traded Canadian corporation, made a grant to the Atlantic Council in 2015. It was——

Mr. SMITH. How much was that?

Ms. BRUTON. It was between $100,000 and $249,000. I would like to give you the exact amount. My understanding is that it is not the policy of the Atlantic Council to do that. If they will permit me to, I will add it to the record.

WRITTEN RESPONSE RECEIVED FROM Ms. BRONWYN BRUTON TO QUESTION ASKED DURING THE HEARING BY THE HONORABLE CHRISTOPHER H. SMITH

The Atlantic Council has received a coveted four-star ranking from Charity Navigator, the premier organization that ranks non-profit organizations across the United States, for its sound fiscal management and its commitment to accountability and transparency. It is the Council's policy to list all of our annual donors on our website and in our annual report, indicating the approximate magnitude and the year of each gift. In accordance with this policy, the Council has already disclosed that Nevsun Resources made a gift to the Council in the range of $100,000-$249,000 in FY 2015.

In response to Congressman Smith's inquiry, I have been authorized to further inform you that the Council received funding from Nevsun Resources in the amount of $105,000 in FY 2015 (the most recent year for which completed financial reporting is available). As noted in my testimony, this grant provided general support to the Africa Center and was allocated at the discretion of the Center's director, Dr. J. Peter Pham. The Atlantic Council fully adheres to its written policy of intellectual independence. For context, please note as well that the Council had an operating budget of more than $25,000,000 and revenues of over $28,000,000 in FY 2015.

Mr. SMITH. If you could encourage them. It does help us to know if there is any financial entanglement.

Ms. BRUTON. Absolutely. Well, and regardless, a six-figure grant is a lot of money. There's no doubt about it. I want to make it clear that the grant was unconditional.

It was general support for the Africa Center. I have no direct relationship with Nevsun. I have not received a raise or a promotion or any kind of incentive as a result of that grant. I do not control the funding.

The funding is controlled by Dr. J. Peter Pham, our director, whose views on Eritrea are in the congressional record and diametrically opposed to my own. My own support for the Eritrean Government goes back to 2009.

In fact, I wrote a piece in Foreign Affairs that the Eritrean Government attached to its letter of protest to the U.N. Security Council when it was sanctioned. So my views have long been on the record and have not been altered in any way, shape or form by Nevsun or by anyone else.

Mr. SMITH. To the best of your knowledge has Nevsun or any of those that they are working with including the Eritrean affiliate supported the Extractive Industry Transparency Initiative, or the EITI? Do you?

We've had hearings on that in this subcommittee for years. We know that DRC, Tanzania, Zambia, and Mozambique are EITI members. Thirteen other African countries are EITI compliant. Ethiopia is an EITI candidate but Eritrea is not. I am not even sure if they are trying and maybe you could shed some light on that.

And secondly, do you have a sense as to the condition of the workers?

When we did Sudan sanctions in this subcommittee, and I was chairman then, we tried very hard to delist a Canadian company that was very much complicit in the crimes that were being committed by Khartoum, and we failed. Wall Street rose up in arms and said, you can't do this. We said look, they are garnering huge amounts of money and they are part of a regime that is committing horrific crimes against southern Sudan, what is now South Sudan— 2 million dead, 4 million displaced.

Greg Simpkins and I were just there 3 weeks ago, almost 4 weeks ago, in Juba. It's a mess. Not the subject of this hearing, but a mess. But we tried to do this delisting and they were a Canadian oil company.

And I am just wondering, this extractive industry, the condition of the workers—is there any monitoring being done? Are any of these kids—are any of these people child laborers? It was Talisman Energy—Greg just reminded me. It just slipped my mind.

So what about the workers?

Ms. BRUTON. I have to say, genuinely, I have never been to the Bisha Mine and so I am not necessarily the best person to testify to the conditions.

I can point you to a written description of Bisha by Louis Mazel, who's been the Charge d'Affairs in Asmara. He visited with a large number of other European diplomats and he, frankly, wrote a glowing report of conditions at Bisha. That's the best that I can do since I haven't seen it at firsthand.

I would also note that the U.N. Commission of Inquiry on Eritrea when it wrote its first report, which I read carefully, contained a number of allegations about the Nevsun mine, which I understand they examined carefully and then dropped from the final version of the report because I believe that they were unable to substantiate them. Again, those are not firsthand testimonials but it is relevant that I can at least point to you.

Mr. SMITH. So you would support Eritrea joining EITI?

Ms. BRUTON. I would, and it is my understanding, again, from the diplomatic community and from conversations with Nevsun that they very, very much support it and are working actively to try to make that happen.

They are also conducting a large number of human rights trainings at the Bisha Mine that I am aware that they are also very proud of and I feel constrained from talking too much about them because there is a financial relationship between Nevsun and the Atlantic Council, at least in the past, and I don't want to be their spokesperson in any way, shape or form. But I would point you toward what's on the record at least.

Mr. SMITH. Let me just ask you with regards to the human rights situation, the State Department's Country Reports on Human Rights Practices is an indictment on a myriad of human rights abuses being committed.

I mentioned the CPC designation based on religious persecution and Father Ghebre-Ab elaborated on just a number of people who are actually incarcerated for their faith and the Tier 3 designation by the U.S. Department of State's TIP office, which painstakingly looks at child and sex trafficking, they're among the worst in the world. Do you agree with that or disagree with that?

Ms. BRUTON. I do not disagree with that.

Mr. SMITH. Okay. I'd like to yield to my friend and colleague, Ms. Bass, for any questions she might have.

Ms. BASS. Thank you.

I would like to ask the panel some of the same questions I asked the last panel. I am really trying to understand the country and so I began by asking what is the ideology that guides the country.

I also asked, in the three categories of higher education, military, and government service, what determines that, to begin with. So is there an underpinning ideology that guides the way the country is organized?

Mr. GHEBRE-AB. Let me try to answer the first question—is there a guiding ideology in Eritrea. Now, looking on the history of Eritrea's fight for independence, during the entire 1970s and the 1980s and even going back to the 1960s, the guiding ideology was Marxism. There's no question about it, and when Marxism fell out of favor, they quietly seemed to abandon it but never officially actually abandoned it and a lot of the policies of the government are still informed.

Whenever they have a very difficult time they—it seems to me like it is a fallback ideology and therefore there is no doubt about it. I mean, they always refer to themselves as a Marxist organization and therefore I don't think anybody can argue that.

Do we see that in its policies today? Yes. It's a fallback ideology always, and I'll tell you something. I look at the publications the organizations put out, especially as it concerns religious freedom.

In many publications, it actually lists the number of religious organizations that it was going to do away with, which it has, and therefore this is not really some unknown ideology.

It is very, very closely tied to Marxism but also it has degenerated, of course, into a one-man rule. There is no question about that.

Ms. BASS. So and both of you were born in Eritrea?

Mr. GHEBRE-AB. I was born and raised—I was born and raised in Ethiopia of Eritrean parents. That's my academic discipline.

Ms. BASS. Oh, I am sorry.

Mr. GHEBRE-AB. My academic interest has always been Eritrea also and until 2003 I traveled to Eritrea extensively. So——

Ms. BASS. Oh, you haven't—you're not able to go back and forth since 2003?

Mr. GHEBRE-AB. No, not since 2003.

Ms. BASS. I see.

Mr. BESHIR. Yes, I was born in Eritrea and I left at the age of 18 and I have been here in the United States since.

Ms. BASS. Are you able to go back and forth or——

Mr. BESHIR. Well, the last time I went was in 2002 as a group of colleagues, the group known as G-13. I have one of my colleagues here Dr. Assefaw Tekeste. That is the group that are trying to appeal to President Isaias to implement the Constitution to reform—to loosen economic reform and, of course, that was kind of brushed off and we were not successful.

This is in 2000, October 2000. It's been, like, 16 years. So this is the last time I have been here.

As to the question about the ideology, there is no ideology. To characterize a totalitarian regime a tyrant, I wasn't trying to beat my head trying to figure out what is the ideology of the Ghadafi or Bokassa or Idi Amin or Saddam Hussein, for that matter. They're just simply tyrants trying to stay in power at any cost.

Ms. BASS. So can you guys answer for me, because I keep asking the same question and I haven't gotten an answer about it.

Mr. BESHIR. Sure. Go ahead.

Ms. BASS. About the three categories and how is it decided who goes where.

Mr. BESHIR. So after the eleventh grade all students go to the Sawa camp where they finish their high school.

Ms. BASS. Right.

Mr. BESHIR. Based on the grade they achieve, which most of them there is a cutoff mark ascertained. They would go to the university or if there is no university there is a technical college where they would go to. But the majority them, almost like 95 percent, go in the Army—some of them as a civil servant in the military.

Ms. BASS. So is it—so it is based on test scores?

Mr. BESHIR. Yes.

Ms. BASS. Some people who don't score well go to the military or if you score well you go to the military?

Mr. BESHIR. No, if you don't score well, you go to the military. You have to have high grades to advance to the technical colleges. But the cut-off is so high and they are very selective. Ninety-five percent of them end up in the military, for a simple reason—because Eritrea doesn't have the capacity to absorb all of them or even a large portion of them.

There are very limited seats at the technical college. So most of them end up in the training—in the Army or being sent as conscripts in the Bisha Mine to work in the mines in Bisha.

Ms. BASS. Okay. So——

Mr. BESHIR. To answer your question, there are also appointments to the government. The qualification is simply on loyalty, especially mid-cadre and upper government.

Ms. BASS. Okay.

Mr. BESHIR. You cannot possibly work for the Eritrean Government if you failed the loyalty test. All the high government officials are very fiercely loyal to the government.

Ms. BASS. Okay.

Mr. BESHIR. How do we know that? From the defection of the minister, the journals, the high-ranking military who defect. We talk to them and this is the reason that the brain drain—a lot of smart well-educated people leave the country. So there is a huge gap—a shortage of technical people who have administrative or technical ability and this is one of the biggest concerns.

Ms. BASS. Okay. Thank you.

Ms. Bruton, you support the Eritrean Government?

Ms. BRUTON. What I—what I think is that saying that I support the Eritrean is—to me, it is vague statement.

Ms. BASS. Okay.

Ms. BRUTON. I don't think that there is a viable alternative to the Eritrean Government and I think that if we want to help the people of Eritrea there are two ways to do it.

One, we can push for some disorderly change of power that is likely, in my opinion, to lead to a situation that looks a lot like South Sudan or Somalia.

Or we can work with the present government to try to persuade them to address some of our concerns, for their own sake.

You asked a question about ideology.

Ms. BASS. Yes.

Ms. BRUTON. I think the Eritrean Government has a very strong ideology. I think they themselves have, especially in recent times, pointed out that their ideology has not been as successful as they would have wanted it to be.

For me, when I look at the situation in Eritrea I see, unfortunately, a very painful limbo and I think that that limbo is primarily caused by the fact that the Ethiopian Army is occupying Eritrean soil.

And it is not only that they are occupying the border. There are assaults on the border. One of the——

Ms. BASS. There are what? What did you say?

Ms. BRUTON. Assaults on the border.

Ms. BASS. Assaults.

Ms. BRUTON. One of them in July was a very serious assault.

Ms. BASS. Yes.

Ms. BRUTON. There are bombings of Eritrean territory that are not reported in the press. The Prime Minister of Ethiopia, Hailemariam Desalegn, has repeatedly promised to invade Eritrea in the Parliament.

This has persuaded Eritrea, not unreasonably, that it is in a state of threat constantly and that is one of the reasons that they have prolonged the national service.

Others disagree and I acknowledge the disagreement. They say well, Eritrea could just ignore the threat and disband the military.

But it is hard for me to see how they could do that, particularly because, as my colleagues have pointed out, almost all the jobs in Eritrea are performed by national service volunteers and transforming those positions into paid private sector and civil service posts takes a certain amount of money.

Ms. BASS. So when you said there is—they do have a strong ideology you didn't describe what the ideology was. Do you agree that it is Marxist ideology?

Ms. BRUTON. It was—it was Marxist ideology in days past. I think that they abandoned the explicit ties to Marxism quite a while ago. But I would certainly characterize it as socialist. They don't call it socialist but that is how I would characterize it, yes.

Ms. BASS. So when you say the community service—government service is voluntary, how do people feed themselves? How do they—they receive no salary? They're forced to work for the government?

Ms. BRUTON. If you were to speak with diplomats or an Eritrean on the street—I've asked a lot of people on the street in Asmara about national service. Some of them have horrific experiences with it.

There is no doubt. I don't question the testimony of any person who, for example, has spoken to the Commission of Inquiry. I am grateful for their courage in coming forward.

But there are also many people that I have spoken who have said things like national service is I go on Friday, I give my boss my paycheck and the rest of the time I do my normal job, or national service is a few hours a day and they drive a taxi cab for the rest of the time.

I am not in a position to be able to say which of those experiences is the norm. But I would certainly point out that anecdotally when I talk to people that is the kind of experience they express.

Ms. BASS. So does the government subsidize parts of life? I mean, how—because the way it is been described is—it is forced labor, it is slavery. People are not paid. So I am just trying to figure out which is it.

Ms. BRUTON. People are very poor and the wages for the national service are not living wages. They are a pittance. They're worse than a pittance.

Ms. BASS. So does the government subsidize or is everybody starving?

Ms. BRUTON. No, there is not that much hunger in Eritrea that I've ever witnessed. The government does provide a voucher that provides for basic goods. If you want to more than that basic basket the cost of goods is very high.

I think people depend, as in other African nations, very, very heavily on remittances and on the informal economy and jobs—second jobs, third jobs—that they really scrape together.

Ms. BASS. So how——

Ms. BRUTON. The economic condition is not good.

Ms. BASS. So how do you explain then the 5,000 folks a month that leave and all of the human rights reports about Eritrea?

Ms. BRUTON. The latest figures that I have seen from the U.N. has been more like 3,000 refugees a month. You know, I can look at that and——

Ms. BASS. That's a lot of people.

Ms. BRUTON. It's still a lot of people. I don't know how many Eritreans really leave. There is a lot of talk, for example, that I have heard confirmed by members of the human rights community that, for example, Somalians, Ethiopians, and Sudanese sometimes adopt Eritrean personas because of the privileged status that Eritrean refugees have in Europe.

Until very recently they've had an automatic asylum preference and that is led a lot of people to say, for example, that they are Eritrean.

I have no idea what the numbers are.

Ms. BASS. Well, whatever the numbers are, why are a lot of people fleeing?

Ms. BRUTON. I lot of people are fleeing because the human rights situation is terrible. A lot of people are fleeing because the economic situation is terrible.

I would point out to you that if you look at Somaliland, which is very close to Eritrea and is known as kind of a democratic oasis in the Horn of Africa, the vast majority of youth leave Somaliland too because they don't have economic options.

Migration is a reality for a lot of people in Africa and Eritrea is no exception.

And I do agree, it is worse because of the human rights situation and the ongoing war with Ethiopia.

Ms. BASS. And just one last question. So what is the human rights situation, from your vantage point—from your viewpoint? What are the human rights abuses?

Ms. BRUTON. I think that all of the human rights abuses that have been described are absolutely real. I think that the question is, and the reason that I asked the question earlier from the intelligence officer who asked is there a government in Eritrea, are these abuses systemic.

Are they the result of deliberate government policy or how much are they the result of poverty, the ''no peace, no war,'' bad behavior by people outside of us or that the government has a poor grip on—what is the relationship between the political side of the government and the military?

We have virtually no knowledge of that. I have no doubt that the military are bad actors. The extent to which their behavior is condoned by the government I don't really know.

I've talked to senior people in the government in Asmara, and I may be super naive, but sometimes I think they really believe that human rights abuses don't exist or if they do that they are very, very few and far between.

Ms. BASS. So you're able to go?

Ms. BRUTON. Yes, and to travel very freely.

Ms. BASS. Did you two want to say something before I close?

Mr. GHEBRE-AB. I would most definitely like to say something. The people of Eritrea who have been victims of the most—I mean, the cruelest power I have ever read about or even seen are—it seems to me like there is an effort to make it look so much better than it really is.

For me, what do we expect government officials to say? These are the very same people who have been designated—who have been designated as having committed crimes against humanity by the United Nations Commission on International——

Ms. BASS. Are you referring to the people that she was talking about?

Mr. GHEBRE-AB. Yes.

Ms. BASS. Is that what you're reacting to?

Mr. GHEBRE-AB. Yes. Let me tell you, I am a priest. I am in contact with the people who have left the country so many times. I've been to Israel a couple of times and have interviewed so many people and know how the people feel and how they have suffered and suffered under this regime.

And therefore this effort to make it look like Eritrea is doing its best and because the President said this and that, government officials say this and that, it does not represent what the people experience and what the people go through at all.

There is an utter poverty precisely because of the policies of the government and something was said about vouchers. The voucher system was designed to control the people.

You get vouchers if you are loyal and if your loyalty is questioned your vouchers are held up, which means that the things that you rely on on a daily basis you are denied.

Ms. BASS. Okay. Thank you. Yes?

Mr. BESHIR. Can I just make a comment? I am just really baffled by Ms. Bruton's statement. I don't know what country she's talking about, really, because every statement she made that is the talking point of the regime. You can read it everywhere. You can read it in the Web site and she has categorically denied that she has association with Nevsun.

Why does she appear on the ruling party's rallies and event in the U.S. jointly with the vice president of Nevsun? I mean, there are pictures of her trying to whip up support for the President attending these events. For me, it is really mind boggling that she denies having any relationship with Nevsun.

As to the comments of the issue of the economic conditions or the social conditions, she's absolutely right. The issue is very complicated and we shouldn't get it right.

The problem is she has gotten it right so many times in the short 18 months she has been interested in Eritrea. She got it right—she got it wrong when she said there is no involvement in Eritrea and Somalia—there is no involvement of support for al-Shabaab.

She got it wrong when she said about the Commission of Inquiry. She has gotten in wrong so many times in the short period she became suddenly interested after Nevsun start funding the Atlantic Council. That's in the——

Ms. BASS. Okay.

Mr. BESHIR. So she's right. It's very complicated and we should get it right.

Ms. BASS. Okay. Thank you very much, and I yield back.

Mr. SMITH. Thank you, Ms. Bass.

I'll just conclude with a few final questions. Dr. Beshir, you, in your testimony, said that since it ended the gold production phase and moved to copper production, which requires more logistical support and infrastructure to export, Nevsun has relied on the Eritrean Ministry of Defense, provided with slave labor for mining and security and transportation services.

You pointed out that every year the Eritrean Government rounds up about 20,000 eleventh grade students 16 to 18 years of age to finish senior high in Sawa military camp afterwhich most, except the tiny minority, are conscripted. The overwhelming majority of the youth are sent to work for the ruling party's companies which supply slave labor to Nevsun and other companies.

And then you go on and your—again, your testimony will be made a part of the record. You point out and remind us of the Human Rights Watch report of January 2013 in which that report said Nevsun's experiences show that be developing projects in Eritrea mining firms are walking into a potential minefield of human rights problems. Most notably, they risk getting entangled in the Eritrean Government's uniquely abusive program of indefinite forced labor, and elsewhere you pointed out the environmental degradation issue which is another one as well.

Could you elaborate on that and, Ms. Bruton, if you could speak to that as well. Hundreds of thousands—whatever the number of young people or any people who are forced to be part of this.

I remember in Burma when an American oil company was very much a part of the junta there in Burma was forcing them to be part of building a pipeline and many of us raised strong objections to that Texas-based oil company doing that.

No matter where it is it is wrong and so the accuracy of the Human Rights Watch report and you also point out WikiLeaks also has some insights on that as well. Could you elaborate on that?

Mr. BESHIR. Yes. The 20,000 number is the high school graduates. This is what I mean—every year there are about 20,000. That's what I meant by that.

There are a couple of lawsuits in Canada filed by former conscripts who are in Canada and some of them the U.S. and in Ethiopia.

I just spoke just last night to the attorney who is representing them to get an update of where the case is and he told me that Nevsun has filed a motion to dismiss the case and they suggested that the case be tried in Eritrea—the same tactic Nevsun has used when asked to disclose financial transactions to the U.N. Monitoring Group. They refer the request to the Eritrean Government and what the Eritrean Government has asked about financial transactions or records about Nevsun they will say well, you have to ask Nevsun.

So there is a case to be decided in the next couple of months if the judicial system is capable of handling this case. There is a pending lawsuit filed by three former conscripts who allege human rights abuse and all the allegations that were listed in the human rights report.

Mr. SMITH. Ms. Bruton?

Ms. BRUTON. I don't want to pretend to know more that I know about mining. But I do want to say that I think you raised a very important concern when you said that Western firms operating in Eritrea run the risk of becoming entangled even if they are careful, at least in reputational damage because of the national service program and that has had severe consequences.

The consequences are that China is taking over, basically. All of the mining projects that are coming online, five or six big ones in Eritrea, are Chinese firms and you may have good opinions of Nevsun or bad opinions of Nevsun but Canadian firms have more to fear from public relations scandals than Chinese ones do and they tend to be more concerned about safety and human rights and other things.

And I personally think that ceding that ground to China is not in the interests of the Eritrean people. I think it would be great to get Western investment into Eritrea because I think that there is a positive influence to be exerted there and it is one that the Eritrean Government will be responsive to because it is investment and that is often the best way to get change.

Mr. SMITH. But, again, all the more reason why EITI ought to be a very serious goal and I don't disagree even this much with the China concern. I chair the Congressional-Executive Commission on China.

China's human rights abuses—Xi Jinping is in a race to the bottom with North Korea when it comes to those abuses and that is manifested all over Africa where they can get away with it.

So but the standard for Canada or the United States or any other country in Europe or Africa ought to be so high for OSHA type protections, for occupational health and safety and a living wage to ensure and certainly no forced labor.

Dr. Beshir?

Mr. BESHIR. Can I just make a quick comment?

Even if Nevsun becomes transparent and we have all this disclosure about corporate responsibility and environmental reports, these are unaudited reports.

There is no civil society. There is no independent verification of what Nevsun or any Western company would claim in the absence of civil society's independent verification.

So that just becomes a useless exercise because all this report that we hear they have been unaudited. There is no third party verifying them. So the notion is the Chinese are coming and we should stay there.

As you have pointed out, the Canadian company is very notorious for human rights violations in the last 20 years. So basically when they call themselves Canadian companies they are U.S. companies operating out of Canada because they escape the strict regulations of the Securities and Exchange Commission so they get listed in the New York Stock Exchange and the Toronto Stock Exchange so that they can access the capital market of the U.S.

But in a sense they are mostly U.S. investors escaping SEC regulations or filing of disclosures and so forth.

So, basically, if you look at the percentage of shares owned by Nevsun, they are mostly U.S.—about 80 percent of them. The reason is the Canadians, they don't have a strong central security exchange like we have here.

Each province in Canada has its own supervisory similar to SEC and often times there is no stringent disclosure requirements either of human rights violations or environmental reports.

Nothing is filed. It's the least required disclosure that the Canadian companies—and you probably know from the history of Talisman in Sudan and other parts of Africa of the notorious Canadian human rights violation in the minefields.

So, to me, it is essentially American companies. Unless they are scrutinized and fully listed in the New York Stock Exchange rather than being cross listed, then we will see more disclosures from Nevsun.

Mr. SMITH. Two final questions, and I will be brief because you have been very gracious with your time—how engaged has the United States been in implementing the boundary commission ruling of April 2002?

Father, that was one of the points. I think you all are concerned about that. When you say the U.S. should reengage are you suggesting, Father, that we have not been engaged—it is been on the side somewhere and crowded out by other urgent matters or are we being robust in trying to get both parties together?

And secondly, what can the United States in the international community do to help Eritrea matriculate from its abysmal human rights record? Are there new policies we need to be doing? The boundary commission, obviously, is one—getting that implemented.

Mr. GHEBRE-AB. The United States. The United States.

Mr. SMITH. But we have a new President coming in January. This President still has a few months to do something. Are there any bold strokes that need to be done by him—by President Obama—and the next President? What would you say if he or she was——

Mr. GHEBRE-AB. Yes. The United States played a critical role when Ethiopia and Eritrea went to war in 1998 to 2000, and in fact it was the guarantor for the settlement of the border dispute and for the ruling.

Once the border commission ruled, the United States simply disengaged and many things can be said about that and we can assign many reasons for that and the Eritrean Government, perhaps legitimately, states to this day that the United States should have remained and should have fulfilled its position as a guarantor.

Since then, the United States has not done much and as has been said by so many people before, one of the reasons that the Eritrean Government has forwarded for maintaining this continuous militarizing of the country was because of the threat that was posed by Ethiopia. Partially that is correct.

But I think, as Dr. Beshir had pointed out, removing that as one of the things that the Eritrean regime uses for its hiding militarized policy will probably enable both countries to pursue fiscal relations in the future is what I believe.

And, yes, on paper it has been settled but on the ground it has not and one of the things that Dr. Beshir said was on 95 percent of the boundary there is really no dispute.

On the remaining 5 percent, if the United States were to be engaged and making sure that this is settled I think it will go a long, long way to create the proper climate for de-escalating the conflict between Ethiopia and Eritrea.

And I have also stated that both countries host armed opposition groups in their respective countries, which is one of the reasons for the continuous conflict between the two countries and one of my recommendations was that both countries cease to sponsor these armed opposition groups in order to destabilize each other.

Mr. BESHIR. I think there is opportunity now. After President Obama visited to Ethiopia a lot of things has changed. Following the events in Yemen, the drone program has moved to Ethiopia.

As you may know, as of last January the Arba Minch base has been closed because of Ethiopia's human rights violations.

So there is an opportunity perhaps for the U.S., as not a guarantor but a signatory of the Algiers Agreement. There could be an opportunity, a window in the short period this administration has, that they can exert pressure for the Ethiopian Government to least demarcate the undisputed area of the border, which is 95 percent.

There are only three areas that are disputed. So, I mean, the Ethiopian ruling party has been very supportive, very sympathetic to the cause of the Eritreans since their independence but yet it has been mind boggling as why that didn't happen.

I am told it is hardliners who want to keep the option. If you have an undemarcated border presumably the Port of Assab could be the Crimea of Ethiopia.

They don't have to have a demarcated border to go to Assab and grab it and declare some kind of referendum. But more so of the hardliners, the Ethiopian opposition, which are also based in Asmara, is this anti-Eritrean view that they have.

They still don't recognize Eritrea as an independent state. They still are against the Ethiopian Government precisely because of its approach or views toward Eritrea.

So the border issue is very important to the Eritrean people, especially for those people who fought very hard for Eritrean independence, the anxiety, the fear of that Ethiopian ambition that always lags in the back of their mind that Ethiopia can any time grab Assab or reinvade Eritrea.

So it is a real fear. It is not an imagined—all psychological fear. So Ethiopia does use it. The hardliners use this fear to maintain this "no war, no peace." So I really urge the U.S. Government to push toward implementing the demarcation of the border.

Saying that, a lot of people say Isaias uses the border issue to stay in power. I do not believe it because Isaias will always have a reason to stay in power, border demarcation or no border demarcation.

Since 1990, when we called for reform and implementation of the Constitution, we were told we have to wait for the declaration of independence. After liberation, then we were told we have to wait to draft a Constitution. Then the border was broke.

So I do not believe that that is what is keeping Isaias from implementing the rule of law or bringing reform because it simply is an excuse. If there is not a border issue there will be other excuses for him to stay in power.

Ms. BRUTON. I am glad to say that we are all on the same page with this in terms of the desperate need to do something about the Ethiopia-Eritrea border.

I think the problem is that, as you well know, the United States is dependent upon Ethiopia for its peacekeeping, as we call it, contributions in Somalia and its peacekeeping contributions in South Sudan and its support of our drone facilities and that makes it very difficult for us to put any kind of influence on Ethiopia. I think it is unrealistic to expect us to change that.

But my concern is that rhetorically we have not defended the border. When Ethiopia—and it admitted that it attacked Eritrea in July—the statement from the State Department was both sides need to behave themselves.

And when Eritrea was bombed by Ethiopian forces last March, there was dead silence. Time and time again, in fact, we've been silent when our allies have transgressed against other countries.

And what I feel afraid of is that Eritrea very justifiably believes that if Ethiopia attacks it, they are alone, and it is that perception that is leading them to be so paranoid about their defenses and that is something we can act on and I hope that we will.

Mr. BESHIR. Just a last comment. I mean, half of African countries have undemarcated borders, have border issues with each other. But they don't go to war. They don't suspend the Constitution. They go about their lives and while negotiating this border issue.

So the border issue should not be an obstacle or a condition for the rule of law or implementation of their Constitution. To me, it is just an excuse for the President to stay in power and nothing else, nothing more.

Mr. SMITH. Is there anything any of you would like to add before we conclude?

Ms. BRUTON. I'd like to thank you for looking at this topic and I really hope you'll consider a congressional delegation and I hope you'll continue to give it your attention.

Thank you.

Mr. SMITH. I appreciate that. Thank you all. We will continue our focus and a trip is certainly something we will very seriously consider.

We do travel frequently—Greg and I and other members of the subcommittee—to Africa. Like I said, we were just in Juba.

But I would also point out that when it comes to human rights I don't care what country it is and, again, as I said earlier, the Ethiopia Human Rights Act finally got passed.

When we lost, the Republicans—the chairmanship—the majority, and Don Payne, my friend and colleague went from ranking to chairman again—we went back and forth a few times—he took up the Ethiopian Human Rights Act—I was his chief co-sponsor—and we did get it passed in the House but it did not get beyond that.

Our resolution, it has many, many findings and, of course, I am talking about the Ethiopian resolution. When human rights are being committed, whether it be in Northern Ireland or anywhere else or in the United States we need to speak out and speak out with a clear, transparent, and bold voice so and that goes for Isaias. It goes for every other country in the world.

So I thank you for your very, very important input. It is a road-map for the future. We will try to do our level best to continue pressing.

I hope the administration does. I hope the new administration, whoever it is, takes Eritrea in a better life for its citizens and a government that respects human rights and makes that a very serious foreign policy and that we reengage, as you pointed out, Father, on the boundary—as you all did in your comments.

So I want to thank you so very much.

Mr. BESHIR. Thank you very much.

Mr. SMITH. The hearing is adjourned.

[Whereupon, at 4:23 p.m., the subcommittee was adjourned.]

APPENDIX

MATERIAL SUBMITTED FOR THE RECORD

SUBCOMMITTEE HEARING NOTICE
COMMITTEE ON FOREIGN AFFAIRS
U.S. HOUSE OF REPRESENTATIVES
WASHINGTON, DC 20515-6128

Subcommittee on Africa, Global Health, Global Human Rights, and International Organizations
Christopher H. Smith (R-NJ), Chairman

September 14, 2016

TO: MEMBERS OF THE COMMITTEE ON FOREIGN AFFAIRS

You are respectfully requested to attend an OPEN hearing of the Committee on Foreign Affairs, to be held by the Subcommittee on Africa, Global Health, Global Human Rights, and International Organizations in Room 2172 of the Rayburn House Office Building (and available live on the Committee website at http://www.ForeignAffairs.house.gov):

DATE: Wednesday, September 14, 2016

TIME: 2:00 p.m.

SUBJECT: Eritrea: A Neglected Regional Threat

WITNESSES: Panel I
The Honorable Linda Thomas–Greenfield
Assistant Secretary
Bureau of African Affairs
U.S. Department of State

Panel II
Father Habtu Ghebre-Ab
Director of External Relations
Canonical Eritrean Orthodox Church in Diaspora

Khaled Beshir, Ph.D.
Board Member
Awate Foundation

Ms. Bronwyn Bruton
Deputy Director
Africa Center
Atlantic Council

By Direction of the Chairman

The Committee on Foreign Affairs seeks to make its facilities accessible to persons with disabilities. If you are in need of special accommodations, please call 202/225-5021 at least four business days in advance of the event, whenever practicable. Questions with regard to special accommodations in general (including availability of Committee materials in alternative formats and assistive listening devices) may be directed to the Committee.

COMMITTEE ON FOREIGN AFFAIRS

MINUTES OF SUBCOMMITTEE ON _Africa, Global Health, Global Human Rights, and International Organizations_ HEARING

Day_ _Wednesday_ _Date_ _September 14, 2016_ _Room_ _2172 Rayburn HOB_

Starting Time _2:26 p.m._ Ending Time _4:23 p.m._

Recesses | _0_ | (___to___) (___to___) (___to___) (___to___) (___to___) (___to___)

Presiding Member(s)

Rep. Chris Smith

Check all of the following that apply:

Open Session ☑
Executive (closed) Session ☐
Televised ☑

Electronically Recorded (taped) ☑
Stenographic Record ☑

TITLE OF HEARING:

Eritrea: A Neglected Regional Threat

SUBCOMMITTEE MEMBERS PRESENT:

Rep. Karen Bass

NON-SUBCOMMITTEE MEMBERS PRESENT: _(Mark with an * if they are not members of full committee.)_

HEARING WITNESSES: Same as meeting notice attached? Yes ☐ No ☑
(If "no", please list below and include title, agency, department, or organization.)

Eric Whitaker, Director, Office of East African Affairs, Bureau of African Affairs, U.S. Department of State

STATEMENTS FOR THE RECORD: _(List any statements submitted for the record.)_

Questions for the record for Fr. Habtu Ghebre-Ab from Rep. Chris Smith
Questions for the record for Dr. Khaled Beshir from Rep. Chris Smith
Questions for the record for Ms. Bronwyn Bruton from Rep. Chris Smith
Statements from Eritrean tourture survivors, submitted by Rep. Chris Smith

TIME SCHEDULED TO RECONVENE _____
or
TIME ADJOURNED _4:23 p.m._

Subcommittee Staff Associate

Question for the Record Submitted to
Fr. Habtu Ghebre-Ab
by Representative Chris Smith
House Committee on Foreign Affairs
Subcommittee on Africa, Global Health, Global Human Rights, and International
Organizations
September 14, 2016

Question:

You testified that the Government of Ethiopia closed publications of the Eritrean Orthodox Church before secular publications. What was it about these church publications that the government found so dangerous so early on?

Answer:

[Response not received by time of printing]

Question:

Young people are providing perhaps the largest segment of those leaving Eritrea each month, but what about older Eritreans who are no longer fit for active national service? What is the fate of those who are unable or unwilling to leave the country in which they have lived all their lives?

Answer:

[Response not received by time of printing]

Question for the Record Submitted to
Dr. Khaled Bashir
by Representative Chris Smith
House Committee on Foreign Affairs
Subcommittee on Africa, Global Health, Global Human Rights, and International
Organizations
September 14, 2016

Question:

According to your testimony, Eritrea uses as many as 20,000 11th graders to work for ruling party companies supplying workers to Nevsun. You describe them as slave labor. Does that mean they are unpaid and operate under conditions in violation of international labor norms? Are these children able to complete high school?

Answer:

[Response not received by time of printing]

Question:

You have described Sudan as the destination for many, if not a majority of Eritrean refugees. What can you tell us about reports that the Sudan government allows Eritrea free rein to arrest those it considered "high value" targets for return to Eritrea?

Answer:

[Response not received by time of printing]

Question for the Record Submitted to
Ms. Bronwyn Bruton
by Representative Chris Smith
House Committee on Foreign Affairs
Subcommittee on Africa, Global Health, Global Human Rights, and International
Organizations
September 14, 2016

Question:

Your positive descriptions of Eritrea's government and its policies are a definite outlier among analysis on Eritrea and its policies and actions. What makes you so certain that your radically different interpretation of the facts is correct and that others are so wrong?

Answer:

It is true that many of my views on Eritrea run counter to those expressed by the Western media and by some activist organizations. That is not especially surprising. The media narrative on Eritrea (and indeed, on Africa in general) is overly simplistic, and the statements of activist organizations are by their nature tendentious. The situation is worsened by the fact that very few of those writing and speaking about Eritrea have actually visited the country in recent decades.

Again, I respectfully urge the Subcommittee to undertake a Congressional Delegation to Eritrea. If you were to do so, I believe you would discover for yourself that my opinion on Eritrea is not an "outlier." On the contrary, my views are reflective of a consensus opinion among the Western diplomats stationed inside of the country, who have also been able to witness events in Eritrea and speak to Eritrean citizens at first hand.

Question:

As you have said, Ethiopia has consistently refused to accept the demarcation of its border with Eritrea, and since 2000, a stalemate has developed where Ethiopia has maintained its refusal to abide by the terms of the agreement that ended the war with Eritrea. Yet you seem to downplay Eritrea's belligerent response to Ethiopia's position. How would you recommend this dispute be resolved so that a clash such as happened this spring doesn't develop into renewed warfare between these two neighbors?

Answer:

It is inappropriate to describe the situation on the Ethiopian-Eritrea border as a "stalemate that has developed." An objective and unbiased observer would note that the border dispute between Ethiopia and Eritrea has been resolved through litigation; a firm and binding ruling has been handed down; and one and only one party to the conflict – Ethiopia – has refused to honor that ruling. Ethiopia's refusal to honor the ruling has not stemmed from any action of Eritrea's – it has been in place from the minute the ruling was handed down. Ethiopia has willfully chosen to violate international law and to illegally occupy portions of Eritrea's territory for the past 15 years. It has also launched multiple and significant attacks on Eritrean territory (including the twin bombings deep inside Eritrea in March 2015). And Ethiopia does not deny instigating a major assault on the border in June 2016, which is believed to have killed hundreds of soldiers and displaced an unknown number of civilians. It is true that both Eritrea and Ethiopia have provided support to armed groups operating in each others' territory. But it is absurd to suggest that Ethiopia and Eritrea are equally complicit in the creation and maintenance of the violent and unstable situation on the border.

Ethiopia has the power to unilaterally resolve this "stalemate" at any moment it chooses, simply by honoring its legal and diplomatic obligations and withdrawing its troops from the border. But there is no action that Eritrea could take to meaningfully improve the situation.

I would argue therefore that I am not at all "downplaying" Eritrea's role in the conflict – my comments merely reflect the fact that Ethiopia is the aggressor nation and must therefore be the focal point of all international efforts to prevent further eruptions of violence on the border. (I would note too that this is a point of view with which my fellow panelists strongly agree, despite our many other differences of opinion.)

It is unlikely that the United States will be able to pressure Ethiopia into surrendering Badme. However, Washington does have the power to easily and dramatically reduce the likelihood of future conflict, simply by responding objectively and proportionately to acts of aggression.

When Ethiopia attacks Eritrea, the United States must object, and it must apportion blame. Washington's committed silence in the face of past Ethiopian aggressions has done significant harm to the region, by fostering an attitude of impunity in Addis Ababa. Washington's "hear no evil, see no evil" approach to Ethiopia's acts of military aggression has significantly increased the likely of conflict between the two nations. And this posture is clearly destructive of broader US security interests in the Horn of Africa.

76

MATERIAL SUBMITTED FOR THE RECORD BY THE HONORABLE CHRISTOPHER H. SMITH, A REPRESENTATIVE IN CONGRESS FROM THE STATE OF NEW JERSEY, AND CHAIRMAN, SUBCOMMITTEE ON AFRICA, GLOBAL HEALTH, GLOBAL HUMAN RIGHTS, AND INTERNATIONAL ORGANIZATIONS

These testimonies of Eritrean torture survivors applying for asylum in the United States have been submitted by the Torture Abolition and Survivors Support Coalition (TASSC) International in Washington DC. TASSC provides pro bono legal services, psychological counseling, case management and advocacy training to more than 300 torture survivors each year. Pseudonyms are used to protect the families of these asylum-seekers who still live in Eritrea.

AMON

I am a torture survivor and asylum-seeker from Eritrea now living in Washington DC. My father was a carpenter who made furniture. I apprenticed with him from the time I was a small child while attending school at the same time.

Like all Eritreans, I had to complete 12th grade at the SAWA military camp. The camp is named after Sawa, a village in western Eritrea near the Sudanese border. Both boys and girls must undergo military training for one year and are forbidden from seeing their families. Military instructors told us we had to always be ready to "protect" Eritrea from an Ethiopian invasion. There is a border dispute between Eritrea and Ethiopia but that is not why so many Eritreans are forced into indefinite national service, almost a form of slavery. The border problem is just an excuse for Isaias Afwerki, the dictator who has run Eritrea for over 30 years, to maintain total control over the people.

Everyone at SAWA has to take a high school matriculation exam. Based on the results, students must follow either the military service or college track. Lately a few can follow a vocational track. When I was there those who scored at least 2.3 out of a perfect score of four – about 15% - could go to college. I was lucky to score well enough to get on the college track.

Most students, however, are forced into compulsory military service which can last for years. **Indefinite military service, not economic conditions, is the main reason why so many Eritreans—5,000 a month -- are fleeing the country.** Some of my friends were among the refugees who drowned in the Mediterranean trying to get to Europe.

After college I worked for various government agencies. I do not want to specify which ones because the Eritrean government might be able to identify me and further penalize my family. My father was imprisoned for six months after I left the country and they closed his carpentry shop. Now my family barely has enough money to live.

Security agents started targeting me early in my life. In 2012 they interrogated me three times for visiting the student center at the U.S. Embassy in Asmara, where I went to learn about applying for graduate studies in the U.S. Agents wanted to know why I was going to the embassy so frequently and accused me of being a CIA spy. That same year Isaias issued a proclamation for "universal military conscription." I would have to join the "People's Army," training 3 hours a day for 3 days a week while doing my regular job in a government office. This is when I decided to escape. It was a big risk since it is illegal for Eritreans to leave the country without an exit visa, which is very difficult to get.

Unfortunately I was caught 30 kilometers from the Ethiopian border with some other escapees. We were beaten and taken by gunpoint to an underground prison called *Hashefray*, Eritrea's worst prison. Hashefray is a large hole in the ground invisible to anyone walking nearby. I was locked in a small cell about 6 feet by 6 feet without any opening in over 100 degrees Fahrenheit.

I remember the first time I was interrogated. I heard the screams and cries of another prisoner being interrogated. The fear and pain began then -- I knew I would be the one screaming and crying soon. Then two prisoners were called to take the tortured man back to his cell. I was beaten and electrocuted by the torturers and forced to spend days in complete darkness. This treatment continued for about two weeks until I was transferred to a cell with two other prisoners.

In September 2013, after suffering a mental breakdown and severe back pain, I was finally released. But then I was arrested again for criticizing the government. I cannot describe here exactly what I was accused of this time because the government has spies everywhere who could possibly identify me. I was put in an underground prison with about 200 other prisoners including many who had tried to cross the border. I could not tolerate this situation anymore, and figured out a way to escape prison and get to Sudan. I eventually got an F1 visa from a US embassy and entered the United States in August 2015.

ABRAHA

My name is Abraha. I was born and grew up in Asmara, the capital of Eritrea. After finishing high school I completed military training at the SAWA military academy. I scored a high enough mark on the high school matriculation exam to enter the University of Asmara, where I studied law.

In 2001 I was one of around 4000 students detained in military camps 100 miles southeast of Asmara. We were protesting against the very low wages the government was paying students in its compulsory summer work program. Because of this I was placed on a "Black List." This meant there was a good chance I could be sent to a "rehabilitation" camp that was really a prison for people who did not obey government orders.

National service with either the military or government is mandatory for every Eritrean citizen from age 18-50. After graduation I did my one year of required national service at the Regional Court in Asmara. Then I was assigned to civilian jobs in law. My older brother is one of the Eritreans who has been in the army his entire adult life—for 18 years in his case. He is still serving with little pocket money and no end in sight. Currently he is near Asmara where he is allowed to visit my parents one month a year. However, when his unit was stationed 500 miles away, he could only visit them once every three years. In theory, members of national service are entitled to one month of leave a year. But in practice, permission for leave depends on the discretion of an individual unit commander and location of the unit.

Women are also obligated to serve. Since 2010 the government has increasingly assigned women to the military rather than civilian jobs. Mostly they have to cook for commanders. They are subjected to unwanted sexual assaults including rape. Social pressure and fear have forced many of them to stay silent and there is no process for them to report these assaults.

Eritrea is like a police state. No one is allowed to leave the country without an exit visa, which is very difficult to obtain. People between ages 18 and 50—who are required to perform national service—must carry a Pass Card authorized by their work supervisor or military commander just to move from one town to another. Because I was on the "Black List" and could no longer tolerate living in such a repressive state, in 2005 I tried to escape to Sudan.

But the military caught me and incarcerated me in a military detention camp located in a town called Barentu, 150 miles west of Asmara. I spent two months in solitary confinement in a small, dark room, 6 feet by 6 feet, with one 20-minute break in the morning. During the first month absolute nobody spoke to me, not even the guards. I had no place to move. Sometimes I would cry, sing a song, sleep for an hour, or pray. I grew up in the Eritrean Orthodox Church and later, belonged to one of the banned Protestant churches. Praying would comfort me a little. Sometimes I heard other people in solitary scream, so loudly that guards would warn them to stop or face even more punishment.

Solitary confinement is very common in Eritrean military and security detention centers, especially for those who try to escape. The government considers almost anyone who tries to leave the country a traitor. Putting us in solitary is also a way to discourage others from trying to escape.

In 2015 I managed to leave Eritrea successfully. I do not want to provide any more details about my arrival in the United States to protect my parents and brothers and sisters back home. They could be severely punished if the Eritrean government finds out where I am.

Finally, I would like to recommend an important action the United States can take to improve human rights in Eritrea. It should speak out more forcefully in support of the UN Commission of Inquiry Report accusing Eritrea of "crimes against humanity" including torture, rape, and "enslavement." The U.S. State Department must go beyond just "urging" Eritrea to limit national service to 18 months and calling for the release of political prisoners. It needs to support referring the UN Report to the Security Council and use tougher language in condemning Eritrea's abysmal human rights record.

Moses

Before telling my story, I would like to thank the House Subcommittee on Africa and Global Health for holding the hearing entitled "Eritrea: A Neglected Regional Threat" on September 14, 2016. Many of us in the Eritrean diaspora, including torture survivors like myself, are grateful that Representatives Chris Smith and Karen Bass want to learn more about the terrible abuses in Eritrea. I knew the hearing had been effective when I saw how much criticism there has been from supporters of the Eritrean dictatorship.

I was born in Asmara, Eritrea in 1983, when it was still controlled by Ethiopia. My father was a businessman until he fell chronically ill in 1977. My mother had to raise me and my four brothers and sisters virtually by herself while she cared for my sick father.

After graduating from high school I had to spend a year training in the SAWA military academy like all other Eritrean youth. I scored high enough on the high school matriculation exam to study law at Asmara University, which has since been closed. Then I was required to do "national service" in a civilian agency. That meant the government decided where I was going to work and how much to pay me.

I entered the university in 2001, right after the end of the 1998-2000 Eritrean-Ethiopian war. It was a very heated time. President Isaias became much more repressive because high-ranking officials and journalists were denouncing him for the terrible loss of life from the war, which resolved nothing. I started questioning government policies after he detained so many of these officials.

My national service assignment was working as an Assistant Judge on divorce, contracts and other civil litigation. I was warned many times to stop criticizing the government. In 2010 I was detained for one week and tortured for refusing to attend a three-month political training organized by the ruling party—the *People's Front for Democracy and Justice (PFDJ)*. I just wanted to be left alone and do my job as a lawyer in the courtroom. But that was impossible – the government wanted to use this "training" as a vehicle to control the population and prevent any independent ideas.

In 2012, Eritrea implemented a new universal conscription program; it created a "People's Army" where almost everyone was drafted into military service. Even elderly men like my uncle, who was almost 70, was forced to patrol the city with a gun and train just like other older Eritreans. The government started telling people there was imminent danger from Ethiopia and we had to be "ready for anything." But it was all a lie. **The real purpose of universal conscription was to force everyone to register for the military so they could hold us hostage as soldiers forever.** (Few people are excused from the draft, such as older farmers in rural areas that the government does not feel compelled to control.)

I wanted to get a passport and exit visa so I could leave Eritrea and come to the United States. I complied with their orders and did what they told me. My assignment was to join other civilians in building a damn without getting paid, a form of "slave labor."

I left Eritrea legally in 2014, but many others are not as fortunate. Thousands of Eritreans escape without legal documents, taking the risk of getting shot at the border, placed in an underground prison for months or placed in solitary confinement like Amon and Abraha. Eritreans constitute the third largest refugee flow to Europe, after Syrians and Afghans.

Why are they leaving? It is not because of droughts like in Ethiopia, nobody is starving to death in my country. It is because of a system of indefinite and arbitrary military service, lack of freedom, and the failure of the international community to pay sufficient attention to its repressive policies. I appreciate that the Africa Subcommittee is taking some steps to change this.